PENGUIN BOOKS
KHUSHWANTNAMA

Khushwant Singh is India's best-known writer and columnist. He has been founder-editor of *Yojana* and editor of the *Illustrated Weekly of India*, the *National Herald* and the *Hindustan Times*. He is the author of classics such as *Train to Pakistan*, *I Shall Not Hear the Nightingale* and *Delhi*. His latest novel, *The Sunset Club*, written when he was 95, was published by Penguin Books in 2010. His non-fiction includes the classic two-volume *A History of the Sikhs*, a number of translations and works on Sikh religion and culture, Delhi, nature, current affairs and Urdu poetry. His autobiography, *Truth, Love and a Little Malice*, was published by Penguin Books in 2002.

Khushwant Singh was a member of Parliament from 1980 to 1986. He was awarded the Padma Bhushan in 1974 but returned the decoration in 1984 in protest against the storming of the Golden Temple in Amritsar by the Indian Army. In 2007, he was awarded the Padma Vibhushan.

Among the other awards he has received are the Punjab Ratan, the Sulabh International award for the most honest Indian of the year, and honorary doctorates from several universities. He passed away in 2014 at the age of 99.

Khushwantnama

The Lessons of My Life

KHUSHWANT SINGH

PENGUIN BOOKS

PENGUIN BOOKS

Published by the Penguin Group

Penguin Books India Pvt. Ltd, 11 Community Centre, Panchsheel Park, New Delhi 110 017, India

Penguin Group (USA) Inc., 375 Hudson Street, New York, New York 10014, USA

Penguin Group (Canada), 90 Eglinton Avenue East, Suite 700, Toronto, Ontario, M4P 2Y3, Canada (a division of Pearson Penguin Canada Inc.)

Penguin Books Ltd, 80 Strand, London WC2R 0RL, England

Penguin Ireland, 25 St Stephen's Green, Dublin 2, Ireland (a division of Penguin Books Ltd)

Penguin Group (Australia), 707 Collins Street, Melbourne, Victoria 3008, Australia (a division of Pearson Australia Group Pty Ltd)

Penguin Group (NZ), 67 Apollo Drive, Rosedale, Auckland 0632, New Zealand (a division of Pearson New Zealand Ltd)

Penguin Books (South Africa) (Pty) Ltd, Block D, Rosebank Office Park, 181 Jan Smuts Avenue, Parktown North, Johannesburg 2193, South Africa

Penguin Books Ltd, Registered Offices: 80 Strand, London WC2R 0RL, England

First published in Viking by Penguin Books India 2013
Published in Penguin Books 2014

Copyright © Khushwant Singh 2013

This book is based on Khushwant Singh's writings that have appeared in *Outlook*, the *Hindustan Times* and the *Tribune* from 2009 and 2012.

ISBN 9780143419488

Typeset in Goudy Old Style by SÜRYA, New Delhi
Printed at Manipal Technologies Ltd, Manipal

To Gursharan

In return for bouquets of lilies and roses

This above all: to thine own self be true,
And it must follow, as the night the day,
Thou canst not then be false to any man.

–*Hamlet*, Act 1, Scene III.

CONTENTS

INTRODUCTION

I am now in what, according to traditional Hindu belief, is the fourth and final stage of life, *sanyaas*. I should be meditating in solitude, I should have shed all attachments and all interest in worldly things. According to Guru Nanak, a person who lives into his nineties feels weak, does not understand the reason for his weakness and keeps lying down. I haven't reached either of those stages of my life just yet.

At ninety-eight, I count myself lucky that I still enjoy my single malt whiskey at seven every evening. I relish tasty food, and look forward to hearing the latest gossip and scandal.

I tell people who drop in to see me, 'If you have nothing nice to say about anyone, come and sit beside me.' I retain my curiosity about the world around me; I enjoy the company of beautiful women; I take joy in poetry and literature, and in watching nature.

And despite Guru Nanak's predictions about a man who lives to my age, I do not spend a lot of time lying down—I still rise at four every morning and spend most of the day sitting in my armchair, reading and writing. All my life I've worked hard; I've been a man of habit and stuck to a disciplined daily routine for over fifty years. That has stood me in good stead into my nineties.

But I have slowed down considerably in the past year. I tire more easily, and have grown quite deaf. These days, I often remove my hearing aid, since the noise of the TV and the chatter of visitors wear me out. And I find myself relishing the silence that deafness brings. As I sit enveloped in silence, I often look back on my life, thinking about what has enriched it, what and who have been important to me; the mistakes I've made and the regrets I have. I think about the precious time I wasted in pointless rituals, in socializing, and spending years of my working life as a lawyer and then a diplomat, until I took to writing. I think about the importance of kindness in daily life; the healing power of laughter—including the ability to laugh at oneself; and what it takes to be honest—both with others and with oneself.

My life has had its ups and downs, but I've lived it fully, and I think I have learnt its lessons.

October 2012 KHUSHWANT SINGH

TIME FOR REFLECTION

My neighbour Reeta Devi Varma has given me a one-foot-high lamp with glass on all its four sides. Inside it is a wax-lit diya. Since it is enclosed on all sides, its flame rarely flickers. At times, it waves gently and then stays still. I sit and gaze at it for hours when alone in the evening. It gives me solace and peace of mind. I am told that this is a form of meditation. But my mind is far from being still. On the contrary, if anything, it is super active.

In my ninety-eighth year, I have little left to look forward to, but lots to reminisce about. I draw a balance sheet of my achievements and failures. On the credit side I have over eighty books: novels, collections of short stories, biographies, histories, translations from Punjabi and Urdu, and many essays. On the debit side is my character. I spend many evenings going over the evil deeds I committed in my early years. With an airgun I killed dozens of sparrows who had done me no harm. I shot a dove sitting on its clutch of eggs. It flew up, scattering its feathers till it collapsed. When I was staying with my uncle in Mian Channu, when their cotton factory was closed for a month, every evening I shot rock pigeons by the score. They were picked up by the children to be eaten. I joined shikar parties and killed many innocent birds. At one organized shooting party in Bharatpur, I shot over a dozen ducks in two hours. No one told me it was a wrong thing to do and also a sin for which there will be no pardon. I am paying the price for my actions as the memory of those innocent creatures haunts me evening after evening.

I have also come to the sad conclusion that I have always been a bit of a lecher. From the tender age of four right to the present when I have completed ninety-seven, it has been lechery that has been uppermost in my mind. I have never been able to conform to the Indian ideal of regarding women as my mothers, sisters or daughters. Whatever their age, to me they were, and are, objects of lust.

Two years ago, I decided it was time for me to withdraw into myself. Some people would describe it as retirement. I chose a hallowed Indian word, *sanyaas*. But it was not *sanyaas* as it is commonly understood, as total withdrawal from the world—I wanted to stay in my comfortable home, enjoy delicious food and my single malt, hear good music and indulge my senses, whatever remains of them. I began with a partial withdrawal: I refused to appear on TV or radio programmes. The next step was to drastically cut down on the number of visitors. Here, I have not been successful. Though much reduced in comparison with the past, they continue to drop in. I welcome those I know well but beseech them not to bring their friends with them. They think I have become swollen-headed and think too much of myself. That is not true; I simply cannot take the strain of conversing with strangers. I no longer give interviews to newspapers and magazines. However, some manage to turn our conversations into interviews. I realize that when, at the end, I am asked 'Do you have any regrets in life?' it is the stock last question. Instead of getting angry at the way I am manipulated to give an interview, the question makes me ponder: 'Do I really regret things I did or did not do?' Of course, I do!

I wasted many years studying and practising law which I hated. I also regret the years spent serving the government abroad and at home, and the years with UNESCO in Paris. Although I saw places and enjoyed life, and, having little to do, started writing, I could have done a lot more of what I was best at. I could have started my writing career much sooner. However, my greatest regret is that I did not have more to do with women I admired but didn't have the courage to have an affair with. So it was six on one side, half a dozen on the other. As Ghalib aptly puts it:

> *Na karda gunahon kee bhee hasrat kee miley*
> *daad*
> *Ya Rab! Agar in karda gunahon kee sazaa*
> *hai.*

> (For sins I wanted to commit but did not,
> give me credit
> O God, if you must punish me for those
> I did commit.)

And since I can't relive lost years, the best I can do is to forget them. Why cry over spilt milk?

As a person ages, of his five senses, four decline with the years; only one, the sense of taste for food, outlasts the others. I know this to be true in my case. The older I grow, the more I think about what I will eat for breakfast, lunch and dinner. Of the three meals, the first two are nominal: a buttered toast with a mug of tea in the morning, a bowl of soup or dahi at midday; but dinner, I insist, must be a gourmet's delight. It comprises only one main dish with a salad to accompany it, topped off with pudding or ice cream.

I have also discovered that in order to enjoy that one meal I must be hungry and have a clean stomach. The meal is best enjoyed alone and in complete silence. This is how our Hindu ancestor patriarchs ate their evening meals. They had good reasons for doing so, and I follow the precedent set by them. Dining in company or with members of the family may help in bonding friendships and keeping the family together, but it takes away much of the taste from tasty food. Talking while eating, one also swallows a lot of air with the food. I also follow my role model Mirza Asadullah Khan Ghalib in his habit of drinking and dining. He took a bath every evening and got into fresh clothes before he fished out his bottle of Scotch whisky, poured out his measure in a tumbler, added scented surahi water to it—and drank in absolute silence while writing immortal couplets in praise of wine and women. He does not record what he ate for dinner.

When I drink alone on an empty stomach, I can feel the whisky warming its way down my entrails. I do not get that feeling when drinking in company. Likewise, when eating in company, I scarcely notice the taste of what I keep shovelling in my mouth. When eating alone, I shut my eyes and turn my inner gaze to what I am chewing and munching bit by bit till it dissolves and goes down my throat. I feel I am doing justice to my food, just as the food I eat is doing justice to me. Never be in a hurry to finish your meal; take your time over it and relish it.

I was, and am, a meat-eater. I believe vegetarianism is against the order of nature because besides herbivores, all animals, birds, reptiles and fish live off eating each other. I like to vary my food. Chandan, my trusted cook of over fifty years, is now too old to try his hand at new recipes. So I keep handy menus of eateries that deliver food home. I try them in turn—Chinese, Thai, French, Italian, south Indian. I also have the telephone numbers of ladies who specialize in different kinds of food they cook in their homes and cater to people who place orders in advance. Ms Arshi Dhupia makes excellent Quiche Lorraine and chocolate cakes. And Claire Dutt does an outstanding job of making anything I fancy, from stuffed roast chicken to plum pudding with brandy butter.

'Tell me what you eat and I'll tell you what you are,' claimed the famous French gastronome, Brillat-Savarin. If I told him the varieties of food I eat, he would probably call me a pig. But I do not hog. What I take is in measured quantities. I fully endorse what Brillat-Savarin claimed: 'The discovery of a new dish does more for the happiness of man than the discovery of a star.' Like Lord Byron I look

forward to my evening meal as I used to look
forward to meeting my dates in younger days:

> That all-softening, overpowering knell
> The tocsin of the soul—the dinner bell.

One final word of caution: make sure you never
overeat. An upset stomach and indigestion
ruin the pleasure of eating.

NO NEED TO RETIRE HURT

What preoccupies the minds of men past their middle age after they have done their day's work and have nothing else to do? Based on introspection, I have come to the conclusion that they think of three things whose proportions vary with age but which are concerned with the basic needs of survival, then with procreation, and after that reflections on their past years and uncertainty about the future.

If they are still working, they first think of how their work is progressing and what remains to be accomplished. They are concerned with their bread and butter, the instinct of survival. Then they think of sexual affairs they have had or wanted to have—that is, basically, the instinct to procreate. And finally, they go over their past—friends they've had, misunderstandings or deaths that ended relationships; and what the future holds for them.

Mohammed Rafi Sauda (1713–81), poet laureate of the Mughal court, thought along the same lines:

Fikr-e-maash, ishq-e-butaan, yaad-e-raftgaan
Is zindagi mein ab koi kya kya karey?

(Concern for livelihood, love for women,
    memories of the past
What else is there left to man in his life?)

Mirza Asadullah Khan Ghalib had much the same thing to say, except that he was obsessed with impending death. He craved for *fursat*—a break from the all-consuming business of making a living, in order to indulge his mind on other things:

Jee dhoondta hai phir vahi fursat ke raat din
Baithey rahen tassavur-e-jaanaam kiye huay

In later life, a man spends less time thinking of his livelihood. Recollections of affairs with women recede into the background, as do memories of departed friends. He begins to worry more about his unknown future. I wonder why nature does not provide a fixed period of time for people to enjoy all that life has to offer before they go. Most people are in reasonably good shape until their seventies. Then the body begins to show signs of deterioration— life becomes a burden to oneself and those around one.

Women go through a change in life around their late forties, early fifties. Menopause can take several months, over which they become edgy, lose interest in sex and put on weight.

Male menopause is accompanied by low testosterone levels, low libido, and usually occurs when men are in their fifties. It is of very short duration, therefore more dramatic and, unless men prepare themselves in advance, can play havoc later in their life.

Visualize the plight of a man in government or private service. His working life is time-bound. He wakes up at a specified time, spends the day at work and returns home in the evening. That becomes his routine for about forty years or so. On his retirement, a farewell party is organized for him, laudatory speeches are made, his bosses give him a memento like a wristwatch and say goodbye to him. He is back home slightly later than his usual time. He gets up the following morning but has nowhere to go and nothing to do because he has been retired. He is still in good health. What is he to do all day long? How does he cope with the time on his hands?

With the defence services, the day of retirement can be more brutal. Unless a soldier gets promotions, he is retired in the prime of his youth with a miserable pension he cannot live on. He has to find another job or an alternative source of livelihood.

Retirement is a difficult point in a working person's life and a crucial time of transition. Those who have not thought about what they will do after retirement have time weighing heavily on their hands. It is therefore important to plan for retirement carefully. There are two key things one needs to think about: health and financial stability. It is wise to start planning early so that one is comfortable post-retirement. Instead of brooding and feeling sorry for oneself, one should use time profitably. Many take to attending congregational prayers in temples or gurdwaras and find spiritual solace and peace of mind. Some descend on friends and relatives for gossip sessions. They murder time. And time is precious. There are hundreds of options open to retired people. If they are short of money, they can take up some kind of business or trade which brings in cash. If they are comfortably off, they can take up a hobby or cultivate an interest: take to gardening or learn a language or take art lessons; or engage themselves in some activity in the service of society, for example, teaching children from poor families, looking after stray animals, volunteering to help the old and sickly.

But to do nothing is to become nothing, and a sure way of hastening the end.

NAYI DILLIWALA

I have been a Dilliwala since my childhood, and the city has become an inextricable part of my life. These days, I often think about how Delhi has grown and changed. I am intrigued at how Dilliwalas have been showing more attachment to their city in the last few years than they have ever done since the partition of the country in 1947. I suspect it is due to the change in the nature of its population.

During the British rule, Muslims accounted for 40 per cent of the population. After Partition, over 30 per cent of them left for Pakistan, but more than that number were replaced by Hindus and Sikhs from Punjab, NWFP (North-West Frontier Province) and Sindh. These new migrants had no emotional attachment to Delhi—all their nostalgia was for the towns and cities that they had been forced to leave. Delhi was merely a temporary refuge for them, and they thought they would soon go back to where they had come from. It was not the same with their children and grandchildren. They cultivated a sense of belonging to the city, an attachment helped by the fact that most schools and colleges organize trips to historical sites in the capital on a regular basis. Over the years there have been many coffee-table books on Delhi with excellent photographs. Around the time of the Commonwealth Games, many publishing houses brought out books and publications on Delhi. These have all led to a keener awareness of the city.

I am almost as old as the city I have lived in for most of my life. When I first came to Delhi, I was barely five years old and there was no New Delhi. I recall there were herds of deer, nilgais and wild boars to be seen in what are now Sunder Nagar, Kalindi Colony and Maharani Bagh.

I saw the new city come up day by day as my father Sobha Singh received contracts to build the South Block, India Gate and much else. Most of the contractors were Sikhs and lived on Jantar Mantar Road. A railway along what is now Sansad Marg was called Imperial Delhi Railway (IDR). It brought stones and sand from Badarpur to what is now Connaught Circus. We often got free rides on the IDR.

My father had many interesting tales about the building of New Delhi. When King George V and Queen Mary came to India in 1911 and announced the decision to shift the capital from Calcutta to Delhi, they laid two foundation stones in what is known as Kingsway Camp, where Delhi University is now.

After World War I ended, a team of specialists came from London and examined the site. They were of the opinion that Kingsway was not a suitable place to build the city. They spent a few days riding around the countryside and decided that Raisina Hill would be the best place to build the Viceroy's Palace, the Secretariat and Parliament House.

It took many people to create the new city of Delhi. First, the rulers provided land and selected an architect. The architect drew the rulers' vision on paper; the contractors collected building material and gathered masons and labourers to put on the ground what was on paper. Engineers oversaw that the architects' ideas were properly executed. New Delhi was one of the world's best-laid-out capitals, with wide roads and lots of greenery.

My father's first job as a contractor was to shift the foundation stones from Kingsway to Raisina. He hired a bullock cart, pulled out the foundation stones, rode on a bicycle alongside the cart and planted the stones at the base of Raisina Hill.

The operation was done in the dark so that superstitious people would not take it as an ill omen. For this job, he was paid the princely sum of Rs 16.

As New Delhi began to grow, its flora and

fauna began to change. Keekars, neem and pipal gave way to jamun, sausage trees (*Kigelia africana*), gulmohar, banyan and other exotic trees that were brought from Africa to line the wide avenues. Within some years, vultures disappeared. Soon after, so did sparrows. Many other varieties of birds became scarce. During the monsoon, we used to hear frogs croaking all night and see fireflies flitting about in bushes. Now we have no frogs or fireflies. We heard the wailing of jackals at night and chowkidars calling: '*Khabardar ho!*' They too have been silenced.

Living in New Delhi was gracious, till Independence. Then, the character and culture of the city changed, with the influx of Hindu and Sikh refugees from Pakistan who flooded the city, and the departure of most of Delhi's Muslims for Pakistan. New Delhi's population trebled or quadrupled. New colonies sprang up everywhere, smothering ancient monuments. Huge parts of the old city wall were pulled down to make way for bazaars—independent

India's new rulers did not believe these were worth preserving, nor did they have time to plan for the future.

The New Delhi I once knew like the back of my hand has now become an alien city in which I lose my way. It has grown out of all proportion, extending from Alipur to Faridabad, from Ghaziabad and Noida across the Yamuna in Uttar Pradesh to Gurgaon in Haryana. Lutyens had planned a city for a few thousand civil servants and staff; now it has a population of nearly nine million; he had planned roads for a few thousand cars, tongas and bicycles; now almost every family has a car or two or three, and roads are jammed from sunrise to sunset and even after. It is a city in which more than twice as many women get molested and raped than in Mumbai.

I don't go out anymore. The last time I had to step out to visit the doctor, I found the roads clogged with slow-moving traffic coming to a standstill every few minutes. It gave me time to look at the changes that had taken place. I noticed that there was a lot more greenery, though there were not many trees in flower—only a second blossoming of laburnums (amaltas) and remains of queen's flowers (jarul). Many walls were covered with purple bougainvilleas in full leafy blossom. All the houses along the route had a look of clean prosperity. No hawkers, no garbage, no street dogs. I felt proud of my city and blessed Sheila Dikshit for doing such a good job as chief minister. The only negative point was the chaotic state of traffic: too many cows, a daily growing volume of cars and two-wheelers on roads which cannot be widened, and flyovers which seem to have failed to reduce the congestion. Something has to be done about this or the city will choke to death. What that something is, I have no idea. I also wonder if in the near future we can have polyclinics with doctors, dentists, opticians and medical practitioners in every locality, within easy reach of people who have no cars and are too old to use public transport.

When my father built Sujan Singh Park (named after my grandfather), the blocks of flats I live in, he didn't think that his sons, their children and even grandchildren would end up settling down here; he had higher hopes of large bungalows with sprawling gardens for them. These flats, designed by a Welshman, Walter George, were cheap, and the government took large chunks of it for a rent of Rs 800 per flat. Even so, many flats lay vacant and my father often gave them to any friend in need. Now it's hard to get people to vacate, and many of them sublet their flat for a rent of up to Rs 1 lakh per month! I like the flat I live in as it's snug, with a fireplace and patch of garden at the back. There is not much feeling of community here, and we know each other by our dogs. We usually meet only when there is a death in one of the flats.

Nizamuddin Aulia, patron saint of Delhi, is

said to have prophesied: '*Hunooz Dilli Door Ast*' (Delhi is a long way away), referring to a ruler who intended to take the saint to task when he returned to the capital. The ruler was killed before he could get to the city. I invoke Nizamuddin Aulia's blessings to protect us and our city from doom.

THE STATE OF THE NATION

My biggest worry today is the intolerance I see in our country. We are a cowardly lot that burns books we don't like, exiles artists and vandalizes their paintings. We take liberties and distort history textbooks to conform to our ideas and ideals; we ban films and beat up journalists who write against us. We are responsible for this growing intolerance, and we are party to it if we don't do anything to prevent or stop it.

If we love our country, we must save it from communal forces. Though the liberal class is shrinking, I sincerely hope that the present and future generations totally reject communal and fascist policies.

If India is to survive as a nation and march forward, it must remain unified, reassert its secular credentials and throw out communally based parties from the political arena.

A state that calls itself secular has no business involving itself in purely religious matters such as pilgrimages. By all means make provisions for the security and comfort of pilgrims, as our state governments do during the Kumbh Mela in Allahabad and the Rath Yatra at the Jagannath Temple in Puri, but it's wrong to go beyond that. State officials have no right to associate themselves with or extend patronage to religious bodies, or to give away public land, property or money to them.

It is high time that the government put a stop to the building and construction of any more places of worship. We have more than enough of them already. The government should also deny permission to use public places for religious gatherings. When a place of worship becomes a site of contention or is misused for political or non-religious purposes, the government should take over its control and management. Priests have vested interests in places of worship because their livelihood depends on them.

We must also drastically reduce the number
of people who wear saffron clothes and call
themselves sadhus. They are parasites who live
on working-people's earnings. Men and women
of religion have often tried to influence public
opinion and the government. We, as a nation,
are superstitious, and it is not uncommon for
the most intelligent of Indians, including
Marxists, to consult soothsayers to find out
'auspicious' times before taking important
decisions. In our country, both superstition
and astrology have religious sanction. I am
allergic to those who believe in astrology and
are dictated by superstition. I feel that those
who hold exalted positions, such as our
Presidents, prime ministers and political leaders,
should not believe in such hogwash. It is
dangerous and backward-looking for a nation
to indulge in such beliefs and practices.

It is also time to reconsider facilities provided
to Muslims going on hajj pilgrimages to
Mecca and Medina. Islam clearly provides that
only those who can afford to travel to these

holy cities should undertake the pilgrimage. Nevertheless, the Government of India provides subsidies to pilgrims who can't pay for their expenses and sends official delegations of Muslims free of cost to Saudi Arabia. There is no justification whatsoever for doing so. Most Muslims I know disapprove of such government patronage and would welcome them being withdrawn. Pandering to any one community or religion is nothing but vote-bank politics. We should have learnt by now that any secular government that meddles in religious matters only burns its own fingers.

If the choice is between an India of the dreams of Mahatma Gandhi and Jawaharlal Nehru on the one side, and those of Vir Savarkar and Guru Golwalkar on the other, and we choose the latter, then India will become a Hindu Rashtra, and this will have dangerous consequences. We will soon have to face serious challenges from across our borders. Pakistan seems to be crumbling faster than we feared. Its government has yielded its north-western territories to diehard mullahs, allowing them to impose barbaric codes of conduct. It will not be long before the rest of the country buckles under their influence. India will be their next target. On our eastern border, Bangladesh seems to be sitting on a time bomb which may explode anytime. We have to be prepared for the eventuality and the influx of more unwelcome refugees. We should keep these things in mind when we vote for a government—it should be one that is able to cope with these impending calamities.

All political parties have manifestos which spell out what they intend to do if they come to power: uplift the poor, ensure adequate supply of clean drinking water, eradicate illiteracy, provide a roof over every head, improve relations with other nations. But once published, these manifestos are put away in party archives to gather dust. They are taken out near the next election time, updated, and then put away again. In actual politics, as it is practised in our country, they mean very little. As election time approaches, leaders of different parties start negotiating alliances to see which one will suit them best. No one bothers about political morality. That is why even the shrewdest observers go wrong in their election forecasts. Lust for power and the lure of money lead to horse-trading. Ministers, earlier strongly critical of each other, can be seen embracing publicly, as parties go out in search of allies old and new. What is the simple-minded *aam aadmi* to make of this confusion? What is he to make of claims by politicians of being do-gooders when what they are all really after are their *gaddis*? When it comes to political morality, there is little to choose among any of the political parties we see around us today.

We are forever moaning about corruption in our country—we are amongst the ten most corrupt nations of the world. Corruption is all-pervasive; there are no miracle cures for a disease which has afflicted our society for ages. But we can find solace in the fact that things are much worse in Pakistan, our closest neighbour and chief rival. There also seems to be a significant difference between the patterns of corruption in the two countries. In India, the creamy layer of the government, the judiciary and civil service, is comparatively clean. It becomes murky in the middle, and it is in the lower ranks that corruption becomes rampant ... In Pakistan, it is the other way round. The top layer is massively corrupt; the middle and lower layers are less corrupt. Also, they have more corruption-related violence than we have. We indulge in character assassination; they dispense with niceties like characters and just get down to assassination.

While monetary corruption has been debated threadbare, a form of the same evil which is more rampant and has not received any attention is *khushamad/chaploosi* or flattery. It takes many forms but the objective is the same—to promote oneself.

First there is flattery by applause. I recall some meetings of Indian students in England, addressed by Prime Minister Jawaharlal Nehru. At the end of each meeting a girl would shout at the top of her voice: '*Tum jeeo hazaaron saal, saal ke din ho pachaas hazaar*' (Live thousands of years and may each year be fifty-thousand-days long). Panditji, who was notoriously short-tempered with his countrymen, lapped up this flattery and looked highly pleased with himself.

Another form of flattery is to first build up a rival and then proceed to demolish him or her as best as they can. Sardar Patel was projected as Nehru's principal political adversary and then people put him down to gain Nehru's favour. So the word 'Patelite' was coined for people who opposed Nehru. This *khushamad* paid handsome dividends. Nehruites came to be regarded as forward-looking liberals while Patelites were portrayed as backward-looking.

Though no money was spent, this sort of 'corruption' served its purpose.

Of all the stigmas that disfigure the fair face of Mother India, the worst is the caste system which inflicts unspeakable indignities on lower castes designated Harijans, Dalits or Bahujans. It is sinful, and more so since we have not been able to wipe out the stigma to this day.

However, things have begun to change. The four people who played major roles in bringing about some change are Baba Saheb Bhimrao Ambedkar, Babu Jagjivan Ram, Kanshi Ram and Mayawati. Of these four, Dr Ambedkar was the messiah. He never forgave Gandhi for granting the lower castes only reservation of seats and not a separate electorate. He played a key role in drawing up the Constitution of India and was later law minister in Nehru's cabinet. Disgusted with the social framework of caste hierarchy, Ambedkar exhorted his followers to opt for another religion and persuaded his community of Mahars to convert en masse to Buddhism. He remains the most respected icon of the Dalits and one of the greatest Indians.

I believe a healthy democracy needs both right-of-centre leaders and socialists to function properly. By remaining a democracy, our leaders feel we have done better than our neighbours—Pakistan, Bangladesh, Burma and Sri Lanka. But everyone agrees that communist China has done much better than us. They have controlled growth of population, introduced fast trains which go almost at the speed of airplanes and launched self-made aircraft carriers. The only explanation for their doing a lot better than us is that they work a lot more than us. This is where I agree with Sanjay Gandhi's motto: '*Kaam zyaada, baatein kam*' (More work, less talk). It is time to cut down the number of holidays we take and increase our working hours.

There is another subject on which I agreed with Sanjay Gandhi. I shared his concern over our population explosion, and continue to do so, though I didn't agree with the methods he implemented to promote family planning ... The past few governments have paid little attention to this problem. We simply don't have enough produce to feed the rapidly increasing mouths, and seem to be heading towards disaster. Coercive methods will have to be introduced: disenfranchise all couples who have more than two children, disqualify them from voting in panchayat, state and parliamentary elections, bar them from government jobs.

Another essential duty of the state is to never abdicate its monopoly of punishing criminals. Crimes unpunished breed criminals. If the

state overlooks its duty or delays dispensing
justice beyond limits of endurance, it encourages
aggrieved parties to take the law into their own
hands and settle scores with those who wronged
them. If we do not learn these lessons now,
there will be holocausts in the years to come.

THE IMPORTANCE OF GANDHI

These days, I often find myself thinking of Gandhi. Why do I admire him and claim to be a Gandhian? Three reasons: Bapu Gandhi never told a lie. Bapu did his best to avoid hurting anyone. Bapu staked his life to uphold principles he believed in, and invariably won.

He was the epitome of the person praised in his favourite hymn:

> *Vaishnavjan toh tainey kaheeye, jo peerh*
> *paraayee jaaney ray*
>
> (I know him as a man of God, who feels
> another's pain.)

Gandhi's birth anniversary is celebrated every year since he was murdered, by the performance of a charade we have got accustomed to seeing on our TV sets and in the pages of our newspapers. Netas go to his samadhi in Rajghat, lay wreaths, sit on the ground for a short while, listen to the chanting of his favourite hymns and return home.

It is a ritual that is performed on his death anniversary as well. Few people want to ponder over the question of whether or not we have even tried to follow the path he showed us.

While I call myself a Gandhian and feel very self-righteous, I have no doubt that if I had turned up at his ashram and sought permission to stay for a few days, he would have turned down my request and ordered me to get out immediately. He believed in God. I do not. He was a strict vegetarian and when he was studying law in London to become a barrister, he spent his spare time propagating vegetarianism. I believe vegetarianism is against the order of nature and am an unabashed meat-eater, including beef and pork. He imposed prohibition on us and had it included in our Constitution. It failed, as it has in any country where rulers have tried to prevent people from drinking liquor. I believe drinking in moderation is good for you; getting drunk is reprehensible. I have always relished good wine and Scotch. He propagated abstinence. I think that sex is extremely important and is the most enjoyable experience in life while he was a great advocate of celibacy. I often tell petty lies to avoid embarrassment and hurting people. Gandhi worshipped truth. He never told a lie, however embarrassing the truth was. He equated truth with God. While the existence of God can be questioned, when translated into truth it becomes a part of human behaviour which is tested for veracity day after day till the very end. That is why millions of people around the world, who pay no attention to Gandhi's commitment to vegetarianism, abstinence from alcohol and sex (except to produce offspring), believe Gandhi was a mahatma, a great soul, who had a new message for humanity; and they are proud to call themselves Gandhi Bhaktas.

I have other grouses against Bapu. He treated his wife Kasturba very shabbily and was indifferent towards his sons. He had other negative qualities, which are too embarrassing to relate. And yet I admire him and claim to be a Gandhian.

Gandhi evolved his values and code of conduct in South Africa. He realized that the most potent weapon to use against an enemy stronger than yourself was passive resistance based on the conviction that truth was on your side; thus was born the concept of satyagraha—truth force. It was to be wielded without any ill will, but with the conviction that the other side would come to see your point of view and lay down arms. However, in order to make satyagraha a potent force, one had to shed fear and, if necessary, suffer humiliation and physical violence. Gandhi was often beaten up and put in jail. There were attempts made on his life and more than once he came close to being killed. He never flinched, and soon the white rulers of South Africa, both the British and the

Dutch, came to respect him and acknowledge his extraordinary moral stature. It was this kind of conduct that gave him the image of a saint.

I admire Bapu Gandhi more than any other man. Of all other past prophets we have no knowledge—almost everything about them is myth or miracle. With Gandhi, we know. He was a living example.

Whenever I feel unsure of anything, I try to imagine what Gandhi would have done and that is what I do.

WHAT RELIGION MEANS
TO ME

God is regarded as the Creator of all life on earth, whatever name you give Him—Allah, Brahma, Rabb, Parmeshwar or Wahguru. If believers tell you that God created life, then ask them: if that is so, who created Him? They have no answer. The truth is that life on earth was not created. It evolved, as did every living creature, and was not created by anyone, by whatever name you call Him or Her. It is not God who created us, but we who created God.

I am an agnostic. However, one does not have to believe in God to concede that prayer has power. Most people in distress pray for help when they are in trouble. 'More things are wrought by prayer than this world dreams of,' wrote Lord Tennyson. I know of a lady faith healer whose simple formula to fight sickness is to chant 'Om arogyam'. Apparently it worked for her; she also claims to have healed many people. You may take recourse to passages from sacred texts: most Hindus turn to the Gayatri Mantra, Christians to the Lord's Prayer or one of the Psalms, Muslims to *Aayat-ul-Kursi* (the Throne Verse) or the sayings of Prophet Mohammed in the Hadith, Sikhs to their favourite passages from the Granth Sahib. And there is nothing to stop anyone making up his or her own prayer. Bernard Shaw was right in holding that common people do not pray, they beg.

On religious festivals, after performing the expected rituals, people should spend a little time—about half an hour—in silence and ask themselves: 'What does my religion really mean to me?' Hindus could do this on Ram Navami or Diwali, Muslims on Eid ul-Fitr, Christians on Christmas, Sikhs on the birth anniversary of the founder of Sikhism, Guru Nanak.

I was born and brought up a Sikh. My grandmother, with whom I shared a room till I was eighteen, spent the best part of the day mumbling prayers. At the age of five I was initiated into reading the scriptures. I learnt my daily prayers and could recite them by heart. I went to gurdwaras to pray and joined religious processions. At seventeen, I underwent the *amrit chakna*, a sort of baptism, which symbolized that I had joined the Khalsa. I began to question the value of rituals and the need to conform to Khalsa traditions while in college. But I went along with them. I took great pains to understand the prayers that I had been reciting. Good kirtan continues to move me, to this day. While at St Stephen's College I attended Bible classes. I was particularly drawn to the language of the Old Testament—the Psalms, the Book of Job and the Song of Solomon. It was later, while I worked on the translations of the Sikh scriptures, and found many references to the Vedas, Upanishads and the epics, that I decided to study them to better understand the meaning of my own Gurbani. My interest in religion led me to read whatever I could on Jainism, Buddhism and Islam.

It was during my seven years in Lahore and my close association with Manzur Qadir that I began to question many religious assumptions. He was a Muslim but did not offer namaz, either at home or in a mosque, even on Eid. Neither did his uncle Saleem, who was India's tennis champion for many years and preferred living like a European aristocrat rather than a Muslim nawab. Being Muslim meant little to them. Neither of them bothered to make religion an issue. I did.

When India gained independence, I gained freedom from conformist religion and declared myself agnostic. Oddly enough, and for reasons I cannot fathom, my interest in religions increased. I studied scriptures of all religions, translated many myself and taught Comparative Religions in American universities like Princeton, Swarthmore and Hawaii.

My interest in religion continues. I think that speculating about where we come from and where we go after we die is a waste of time. No one has the foggiest idea. What we should be concerned about is what we do in our lives on earth. An Urdu verse sums it up neatly:

Hikayat-e-hastee sunee
To darmiyaan say sunee;
Na ibtida kee khabr hai
Na intiha maaloom

(What I have heard of life
Is only the middle;
I know not its beginning
I know not its end.)

Although I do not practise religious rituals, I do have a sense of belonging to the Sikh community. Whatever happens to the Sikh people is of concern to me and I speak up or write about it.

I have imbibed what I think are the basics of Sikhism as I see it now.

I regard truth to be the essence of religion. As Guru Nanak said:

Suchchon orey sab ko
Ooper Suchh Aachaar

(Truth above all
Above truth truthful conduct.)

I do my best not to lie. It is easier sticking to the truth than telling lies because lying requires cunning to cover up lies you have told before. Truth does not require brains.

Earn your own living and share some of it with others, said Guru Nanak:

> *Khat ghaal kichh hathhon dey*
> *Nanak raah pachchaney sey*

> ('He who earns with his own hands and with his own hands gives some of it away,' says Nanak, 'has found the true way.')

I try not to hurt others' feelings. If I have done so, I try to cleanse my conscience by tendering an apology.

I have also imbibed the motto: '*Chardi Kala*'— 'Ever remain in buoyant spirits, never say die.' It is worth pondering over. It is worth trying out.

URDU POETRY, MY PASSION

I have an abiding passion for Urdu poetry and have been translating it almost all my life. My novel *Delhi* has Urdu verse in it. I have translated Iqbal's 'Shikwa' and 'Jawab-e-Shikwa' and have collaborated on two collections of Urdu poetry.

Unfortunately, Urdu is a language that's dying in the land where it was born and where it flourished. The number of students who take it as a subject in schools and colleges is dwindling. Apart from Kashmir, where it is taught from the primary to the postgraduate levels, in the rest of the country it is a second or third language. Knowledge of Urdu doesn't ensure getting jobs, while knowledge of English, Hindi or other regional languages does. Those who write Urdu in the Arabic script refuse to admit that it can be easily read in Devanagri or Roman script, and Hindi purists refuse to include Urdu poetry in school and college textbooks. As a result, Urdu is dying here while it continues to be nurtured and flourish in Pakistan, where it is the national language, preferred to the more commonly spoken Punjabi and Sindhi.

Urdu (which literally means 'camp') has a mixed linguistic heritage, which is why it is such a rich language. It evolved as a mixture of Turkish, Arabic and Persian, spoken by the Muslim soldiers of the invaders' armies, and Sanskrit, Hindi, Braj and Dakhani of the Indian soldiers in the Mughal military encampments. It was also known as Rekhta in Mir and Ghalib's time. The educated elite, who preferred to write and speak in Persian, looked upon the language with some disdain. It was the same with poets right up to the time of Iqbal. They all wrote in Persian until they realized that Urdu was more popular with the masses and gave them a much larger audience.

While most Urdu poets were and are Muslims, to whom wine is haram, they write more about the joys of drinking than on almost any other subject. Urdu poetry is full of references to the *maikhana* and the *saqi* though both seem to be figments of the poets' imaginations. Much of Urdu love poetry was addressed to courtesans, whose *mehfils* the poets patronized. A lot of it was also addressed to rosy-cheeked, round-bottomed boys who often acted as wine servers. Other stock images from Arabic and Persian art and literature dominate Urdu verse: the nightingale's lament for the rose; moths incinerating themselves on flames; Majnu's quest for his beloved Laila. Along with overwhelming romance, there is an obsession with the decline of youth, and death. But apart from themes of despair, there is also plenty of wit and humour.

The most popular form of Urdu poetry is the ghazal, and Hindi films—music composers and playback singers—have had a great role to play in popularizing Urdu verse. Above all, it is they who have made Urdu known to millions who do not even know that the language is written from right to left.

GHALIB, THE GREATEST OF
THEM ALL

The greatest Urdu poet, and one to whom I turn again and again, is Ghalib. Mirza Asadullah Khan Ghalib was born in Agra on 27 December 1797. His father and forefathers were Seljuk Turk soldiers of fortune who sought employment in the armies of princes. His father married into a distinguished and prosperous Agra family but died when Ghalib was just five. Ghalib spent most of his childhood in his maternal grandparents' home and received education in Persian, Arabic, Urdu, logic and philosophy. He started writing in Urdu at a very young age and in Persian when he was eleven. He grew into a handsome youth, married in his teens and had several children, none of whom survived.

Unlike his ancestors, Ghalib decided to live by the pen rather than the sword. Since the royal court was in Delhi, he moved there to seek the patronage of Emperor Bahadur Shah Zafar, himself a poet of some calibre, and the *umrah* (nobility) who frequented the palace. Ghalib also sought favours from the British in Calcutta and Queen Victoria in London. Poets could not survive on poetry alone, he pointed out, so rulers owed it to them to keep them in comfort. In a letter to the queen, Ghalib wrote that the kings of Persia 'would fill a poet's mouth with pearls, or weigh them in gold, grant them villages in fief or open the doors of their treasuries to . . . him'. Ironic that a man who so greatly enriched Persian and Urdu literature remained a beggar all his life.

Ghalib was a nonconformist and a bon viveur. Though he revered Allah and the Prophet, he never said his five daily prayers, never fasted during Ramzan, never went on pilgrimage to Mecca. He patronized houses of pleasure, consorted with courtesans and was inordinately fond of liquor. He preferred French wines or rum but also liked Scotch, which he imbibed every evening while he composed poetry. When someone warned him that the prayers of persons who drank wine were never granted, he said: 'My friend, if a man has wine, what else does he need to pray for?'

When a Hindu friend brought him a bottle, Ghalib thanked him in verse:

> Long had I wandered door to door
> Seeking a flask of wine or two—no more
> Mahesh Das brought me that immortal
>   draught
> Sikander spent his days seeking for.

Ghalib gained a reputation as a man of ready wit and clever repartee. Hali mentions a dialogue between Ghalib and the king, who was very particular about fasting during Ramzan: 'Mirza, how many days' fast did you keep?' asked the king. Ghalib, who had not fasted at all, gave a reply with a double meaning: 'My lord and my guide, I failed to keep one.' After the 1857 mutiny had been put down, the British drove most Muslims out of Delhi. Ghalib, who had no sympathy for the mutineers, stayed inside his home while it lasted. Once the British had taken control of Delhi, he was summoned by a Colonel Burn and asked, 'You a Muslim?' Ghalib replied, 'Half. I don't eat pork but I drink wine.'

Next to alcohol, Ghalib loved mangoes. During the season he'd eat up to a dozen every day. Hali recounts an incident when the poet was strolling with the emperor in the palace orchard and kept staring at the mango trees laden with fruit. The king asked, 'Mirza, what are you looking at so attentively?' Ghalib said, 'My lord and my guide, some ancient poet has written: "Upon the top of every fruit is written, clearly and legibly, this is the property of A, the son of B, the son of C." And I am looking to see whether any of these bears my name and those of my father and grandfather.' The king had a basketful of his finest mangoes sent to him the same day.

Throughout his life Ghalib lived a hand-to-mouth existence, ever short of cash, ever living on credit. He was also a gambler and once spent three months in jail for running a gambling den.

It's strange that Ghalib initially thought that deep emotions could not be expressed in Urdu and preferred to pen them in Persian. Fortunately, he changed his mind in time and left a veritable treasure house of gems. They lose much of their lustre in translation. The meaning comes across but the music of the words is lost.

Ghalib tried to forecast the year of his demise but went woefully wrong in his guess. He died in 1869. He was closer to the truth when he wrote:

> Life gallops on at a reckless pace
> I know not where it will stop
> The reins are not in my hands
> My feet not in the stirrups.

THE BUSINESS OF WRITING

The world of writers and publishers has changed beyond recognition. The pioneers among Indians writing in English—Mulk Raj Anand, R.K. Narayan and Raja Rao—either had patrons who helped them find publishers or organizations which sponsored their works. They made some noise in literary circles but not much money. The institution of literary agents was little known. The only one I had heard of in my days was Curtis Brown. It was said that if they took up your work, they would find you a good publisher and take their cut on royalties due to you. I for one never went through a literary agent. Neither did I have any problems finding a good publisher. I was happy with the 8 to 10 per cent royalty they gave me on the sales of my books. Today a literary agent has become a powerful factor in publishing: the best of writers use them because it is they who get publishing houses to cough up huge sums as advance royalties. The whole business resembles a whorehouse. Publishers can be compared to brothel keepers; literary agents to *bharooahs* (pimps) who find eligible girls and fix rates of payment; writers can be likened to women in the profession. Newcomers are *naya maal* (virgins) who draw the biggest fees for being deflowered. Advance royalties being paid these days run up to Rs 50 lakh, sometimes even before a word of the projected work has been written. Advances offered to authors in India are often higher than those offered in America or England or in any other European country. But they are offered only for works in English, not for works in our regional languages.

These days publishing houses take great care to package their books with catchy, saleable titles, and beautiful jackets carrying a line or two by a celebrity author vouching for the excellence of its contents. It has become a racket. It's no better than those who sell their wares in Kolkata's Sonagachi, Mumbai's

Kamathipura and Hyderabad's Mehboob ki Mehendi.

It was during British times that some Indians took to writing literary works in English. Among the pioneers, Raja Rao could be witty, until he assumed the role of a guru imparting ancient wisdom to his disciples. R.K. Narayan stuck faithfully to his Malgudi tales and became the icon of Karnataka and Tamil Nadu. The new Indian writers are much more at ease with the English language. The Jhumpa Lahiris and the Arundhati Roys of today are much better writers than the R.K. Narayans and the Raja Raos of the past.

No sooner does an Indian writer, hitherto unknown, win a prestigious international literary award like the Booker or the Nobel, than he or she soars skywards like the mythical flying horse Pegasus and is seen by earthlings as an astral phenomenon, an awesome manifestation of the divine. Every time it neighs, they construe it as a message from the divine. Even if it drops a turd, it is regarded as manna sent by the gods.

We saw this happen to V.S. Naipaul, Salman Rushdie and Arundhati Roy. We've seen it happen more recently to Aravind Adiga. No one had heard of him till his novel *The White Tiger* won the Booker. Hot on the heels of the award came his collection of short stories *Between the Assassinations*. It is worth remembering that Adiga wrote the stories first but couldn't find a publisher till after he had written his novel. In many ways, his stories were a precursor to *The White Tiger*: similar characters reappear in different forms and incidents are repeated with minor differences. They actually make better reading than the Booker Prize–winning novel.

WHAT IT TAKES TO BE A WRITER

I am not a learned man. I am as far removed from being a scholar as anyone could be. I was a poor student, a briefless barrister, a tactless diplomat and ended up as an ill-informed journalist. So I was amazed when some pressmen in Bangalore pronounced that I was the Dronacharya of Indian journalism.

I did no reading in school and college. It was later, when I was doing law and in the diplomatic service, where I didn't have much work to do, that I began reading in a serious way. For the last fifty years, I've read maybe two or three books a week. With works of fiction, there are not many you want to read again from beginning to end. I go back to poetry, prose that comes close to poetry, blank verse, Shakespeare's plays. I keep *The Oxford Book of English Verse* by my bedside and travel with it. There's a lot of Urdu poetry I return to, and poems like Eliot's 'The Wasteland', which I must have read about forty times.

What draws me to poetry is the language, the music of words, the terseness. The essence of good literature is poetry. And the best example you'll find of good literature, where many sections are so tightly written that there's not a word you can change, is the Bible. I read the Old Testament over and over again.

What I do have is a reasonably good memory for poetry. I can dish out couplets and at times an entire verse by rote. People around me get impressed and get deluded that I am a man of learning which, I repeat, I am not.

The other day I was going through *A Collection of Familiar Quotations* by John Bartlett (The Wisdom Library), which I had bought over thirty years ago in Honolulu when I was on a teaching assignment at the University of Hawaii. It is heavily marked as I have gone over it many times.

I came across two lines by Edward Young (1681–1756) under the title *Love of Fame*. They made me wince.

Some, for renown, on scraps of learning
dote,
And think they grow immortal as they
quote.

At school, I was hopeless at all subjects. And although I was very keen on sports, I wasn't any good at games either. The only bright point was a comment from my English teacher in my report card. Miss Budden, who had come from England to teach in Modern School for two years, wrote that I had the possibility of making it as a writer. Even then, I was a good storyteller, the family jester, narrating events with a punchline in a way that none of my brothers could. The comment from Miss Budden more than amused my father, who had already decided that I was going to be a lawyer because I was such a chatterbox.

An editor once said I had turned bullshit into
an art form. So I said, 'You try it—it's very hard
work.' I have never taken myself too seriously.
I think this has helped me speak and write
freely, without worrying about what people
might think and how they might react. Frankly,
I don't give a damn. I never have. I have never
deliberately sought controversy or wanted to
create trouble. I've always wanted to be true to
myself and write honestly.

I have never rated myself very highly as a
writer. I can tell good writing from the not so
good, and first-rate writing from the passable. I
know that of Indian writers or those of Indian
origin the late Nirad Chaudhuri, V.S. Naipaul,
Salman Rushdie, Amitav Ghosh and Vikram
Seth handle the English language better than I
do. I also know that I can and have written
as well as R.K. Narayan, Mulk Raj Anand,
Manohar Malgonkar, Ruth Jhabvala, Nayantara
Sahgal and Anita Desai.

Two writers who had a huge impact on me
when I was young were Aldous Huxley and

W. Somerset Maugham. Their work left a deep and lasting impression on me.

When I think of the major Indian novels in the last sixty years that have left a deep impression on me I'd say, in no particular order:

V.S. Naipaul's *A House for Mr Biswas*

Salman Rushdie's *Midnight's Children*

Vikram Seth's *A Suitable Boy*

Amitav Ghosh's *Shadow Lines*

Kiran Nagarkar's *Cuckold*

Arundhati Roy's *The God of Small Things*

Jhumpa Lahiri's *Interpreter of Maladies* (this is a collection of short stories)

I. Allan Sealy's *The Trotter-Nama*

Jaysinh Birjepatil's *Chinnery's Hotel*

Anita Rau Badami's *The Hero's Walk*

Tabish Khair's *Filming: A Love Story*

M.G. Vassanji's *The Assassin's Song*

A question that I am often asked is how does one become a good writer.

Writing is often therapy for a troubled soul. But you have to be born a writer. No school or classes can teach you how to become one. There has to be something in you, a compelling urge. And you have to keep at it. The motivating force cannot be money (for there is much more money to be made running a gas station or practising law or medicine). And you are extremely lucky if you can write both fiction and non-fiction with equal ease and prowess.

Writers have different styles and each writer is unique. They can be temperamental, have their quirks and eccentricities. They can be moody and dislikeable; they can be warm and kind human beings. Usually, writers are an interesting and colourful bunch—though I can think of a few who are crashing bores.

To be a good writer, you have to be totally honest and not afraid to speak out. You have to have the ability to work hard and the stamina for a long haul. Sometimes you will sit for hours staring at a sheet of blank paper in front of you. You will have to have the determination not to get up till the sheet is filled with writing. It doesn't matter if you fill it with rubbish. The discipline will prove worthwhile.

Practise as much as you can. Keeping a diary, writing letters, emails—even that is good exercise.

Along with hard work, read whatever you can—whether it's the classics or fairy tales or even nonsense verse. Reading will make you capable of distinguishing between bad and good writing. There is no substitute for reading. This is also the only thing that expands your vocabulary.

Moreover, one should never be pompous or pretentious. Don't show off by using difficult words. That comes in the way of communicating with the reader.

Always do your homework. A writer's responsibility—whether he's an essayist or a novelist—is to inform his reader while he provokes or entertains him. The challenge is to tell him something he doesn't know. And don't talk down to your reader; level with him.

We read history to learn about the past, and pass exams. We read biographies and autobiographies to acquaint ourselves with the lives of great men and the times they lived in. We read fiction for amusement. At times, we are lucky enough to come across a book which combines history, biography and fiction, from which we learn about our past and present, and which we enjoy reading.

It is tempting to write one's life's experiences. A first novel is very often autobiographical. However, non-fiction is a different ball game altogether. Memoirs of retired generals and civil servants rarely make for good reading. They are so full of their own achievements that they not only make their readers feel inadequate, they also end up being terribly boring. What is permissible in a biography is not suitable for an autobiography.

Very few people write history the way history should be written: not as a catalogue of dry-as-dust kings, battles and treaties, but by bringing the past to the present, putting life back in characters long dead and gone, in order to make the reader feel he is living among them, sharing their joys, sorrows and apprehensions.

Above all—and I'm repeating this because it is so important—don't be afraid to be yourself and to be honest. If you write fearlessly and candidly you have to be prepared to pay the price. It's because of my writing that I got the reputation of being a dirty old man but it's never bothered me.

I've always written what I felt and believed to be true. I bared all in my autobiography—if I hadn't, there wouldn't have been any point in writing it. If you write, then you also have to be prepared for criticism. I have never felt like giving it back to my critics, because I'm not vengeful. In my writing, I've always tried to follow my motto: inform, amuse, provoke.

I'm lucky that I've been able to continue writing into my nineties. My eyesight's good and I keep up with my reading as well. The thing is, I don't know how to sit and do nothing. So I can't stop! I don't know how

many of my books will be read after I'm gone.
As Hilaire Belloc said:

> When I am dead, I hope it may be said:
> 'His sins were scarlet, but his books were
> read.'

JOURNALISM THEN
AND NOW

I was teaching courses on Comparative Religions and Contemporary India in the US when I decided to accept the offer of editorship of the *Illustrated Weekly of India*. It was 1969 and the job was in Bombay. The *Illustrated Weekly* was at that time the only magazine of its kind, and I wanted to try my hand at journalism. I had worked earlier with All India Radio as well as *Yojana*, a magazine brought out by the government, and I had been writing regularly for foreign journals like the *New York Times*. I was also writing 'middles' for Indian papers—the *Statesman* regularly and the *Times of India*—so my byline was not totally unknown to people. I wrote what I felt, what I thought about, and what I'd seen and observed. I used to travel a lot so there was always a lot to write about.

I was able to make a success of the *Illustrated*

Weekly because I had no baggage. I came to it with a clean slate. I was very clear about what I wanted to do and what I had to do. I have never made any distinctions between journalism and literature. They're both about communication. I had no problems writing about politics because I had opinions and I wasn't scared to air them.

I was full of self-confidence, and belief in my three-pronged formula of 'inform, amuse, provoke'. Because my teaching stint in America had made me aware of how little I knew about the people of India, I had read and learned a lot about different castes and communities, and this now stood me in good stead. I was lucky I had no real boss and so was given a free hand. We began with a series on the people of India—different communities—and then one called 'I Believe' where celebrities talked about various topics: God, corruption, destiny, religion, among other things. We had articles covering current issues. And features celebrating the lives of great men—Jain Mahavir's birth anniversary, for example. I wrote to chief ministers of various states saying honouring his life wasn't enough—you must practise what he preached, do something concrete. And if they were willing to do that I would give them all the publicity that they wanted. The response was terrific. Many of them banned shikar in their state. We covered it in the magazine. We also published provocative pictures with very detailed captions that legitimized the pictures— a still from the film *Siddhartha* with Simi Garewal wearing very little; a tribal girl with information about her tribe, that sort of thing. And circulation shot up. There was no looking back.

In my time, the editor was really the boss of his newspaper or magazine. Now there are national newspapers with all-India circulations like the *Times of India* and the *Hindustan Times*, but I do not even know the name of the editor because he no longer runs the paper—it is either the proprietor or the proprietor's children. The papers carry as much news as they can squeeze in on the front page—that is, if the front page isn't an advertisement. In the rest of the paper, what dominates is Bollywood or fashion designers, exotic food, restaurants and pretty girls. Take a look at all the papers— they are pretty unreadable.

These days I don't think any editor makes much of a difference to a daily paper because, apart from reports from correspondents in different parts of the country and the centre page which carries editorials and columns, more than half the content of a paper consists of material from wire services or syndicated features from foreign journals, and the Page-Three kind of froth. I go through about six to eight newspapers everyday and most of my time is spent doing crossword puzzles because that's usually the most interesting thing I find in newspapers today.

Many editors today like to preach, and care little about presenting facts objectively. They are often both pompous and pedantic. It was not so in the past. Names like Frank Moraes, Kasturi Ranga Iyengar, Pothan Joseph and Prem

Bhatia had credibility with readers. Dileep Padgaonkar, editor of the *Times of India* in the eighties, was not very wrong when he said that next to the prime minister he had the most important job in the country. Constructive criticism of the ruling party came not from the opposition but from the free press edited by able, responsible men—people like S. Mulgaonkar. He was a great editor, handled the language with great skill and was highly readable. B.G. Verghese was outstanding—he might have been too stolid, but he was very honest and straightforward. Frank Moraes had impeccable integrity, and an excellent command of the language.

The scenario changed with television. Television posed a serious challenge because of its enormous reach. We are a lazy people. Once you've watched something on the TV screen, you don't want to read about it in the next morning's paper. There is a fatigue that sets in. With the growth of 24x7 TV news channels, fewer and fewer people bothered to read editorials. Proprietors of newspapers realized that editors were dispensable and they could find other ways to meet the challenges posed by TV and the electronic media. Which is why newspapers began filling their pages with filmi gossip, society parties and the like.

The challenge for the print media today is to make subjects readable—subjects such as current affairs, politics, culture. You have to spend time studying the subject and then have the ability to put it across in language that people understand. But the problem is, there are not enough journalists who are interested in specializing, and most of them are therefore not equipped to write on the subjects they cover. They don't do their homework either—they just can't be bothered. That's why so much of the content of newspapers now consists of banal reports of speeches or political meetings. Articles these days are riddled with clichés and Indianisms. The writers' command of the language is poor. That's because journalists these days aren't well read. You have to be able to hold the reader's attention. If you can't capture the reader's interest in the first few lines, then you've lost him.

A good magazine or newspaper should be a cocktail of different things. I don't much care for listings of best schools and colleges that keep appearing nowadays with alarming regularity. I find these listings both dubious and tedious. What would be more interesting and useful would be regular surveys of the achievements of our various states. There should also be more pieces on subjects like the green revolution, which for most Indians is associated only with wheat and rice. But what about floriculture or horticulture—the prospects for growing fruit like kiwis, avocados or macadamia nuts, or cultivating orchids and exotic lilies. Readers would surely find such articles of interest, as would entrepreneurs; and agricultural universities would be provoked into doing research on these.

The pictorial content of a journal is also of utmost importance, as important as the text. A picture too needs to inform, amuse and provoke. Journalists today tend to overlook the importance of captions—an incomplete or incorrect caption can destroy the impact of a photograph.

It is now a very competitive market, so you have to constantly think of your audience. Who are your readers? What are their interests? How intelligent are they? Magazines, for instance, need to be a little more serious, and certainly more amusing than they are these days. Indians lack a sense of humour. We tend to rely too much on strip cartoons taken from foreign syndicates when we have perfectly competent cartoonists of our own. Why can't we have our own Dennis the Menace, for instance?

Another thing which might add to a magazine's readability would be articles critical of religious practices, astrology, horoscopes, superstitions etc. Most of these beliefs are totally irrational. Religion has become a menace in this country. Take the Kumbh Melas—huge state resources are spent to prevent the stampedes that take place. Crores of rupees are given to Muslim pilgrims to perform hajj. Of course, articles criticizing these practices would be highly provocative as religion is a sensitive subject and a very important part of Indian life. But there are ways of putting things across without having the Shiv Sena burn down your office.

Breaking a news story is the thing now—whether it's on television, or scoops and sting operations conducted by magazines and newspapers. These are important, and I believe a journalist is justified in using whatever means he or she can to expose those who profess one thing and do something entirely different. There is far too much skulduggery in today's world and it's the duty of journalists to expose it. Of course, it is important that the journalist must be strictly above board—there have been instances in the past where journalists have ended up as blackmailers. But I'm all for sting operations for the sake of the larger common good, for the sake of public morality.

While every citizen has the right to privacy and anyone who invades it deserves to be punished, a distinction should be drawn between a private citizen and persons in public life, such as politicians, civil servants, defence personnel, members of the judiciary, leaders of religious organizations, business tycoons and others who preach public morality. And if what they profess in public does not correspond with what they are practising themselves, and if they are cheating the nation or indulging in corrupt practices, then exposing them through sting operations is wholly justified.

One tactic that the print media often employs in order to get new readers is to change its look. Meddling too much with the layout of a newspaper or magazine can be very disturbing. It makes the reader very uneasy. Newspapers and weeklies are things of habit and there's a comfort factor for the reader who becomes used to seeing the pages arranged in a particular way. If one has to make changes they should be done subtly and cleverly. Very often, expensive designers are brought in from outside and hired to change the look completely. They make radical changes. When the changes are too drastic, you are sure to lose your readers.

THINKING ALOUD

On Partition

Indians have never had an integrated society. Besides caste and language divisions, the greatest barrier has been the Hindu–Muslim divide. Hindus and Muslims have got along reasonably well but have always kept their distance from each other. There has never been any real integration—by way of families mixing, visiting each other's homes, and contemplating matrimonial relationships. The British fostered the feeling of separateness between the two. As the time neared for the British to leave, Muslims began to feel uneasy at the prospect of living in a Hindu-dominated India.

Years before Partition, Lala Lajpat Rai had made a rough map dividing India along communal lines. Later, Chaudhry Rehmat Ali coined the word 'Pakistan'. Allama Iqbal, who at one time composed patriotic verses including

Saarey jahaan se achchha, spoke of a Muslim state. Jinnah's contribution to separateness was evolving the two-nation theory—that Hindus and Muslims were two separate nations which could not live together in one state. But long before Jinnah had come up with the two-nation theory, it was people like Keshav Baliram Hedgewar, Bal Gangadhar Tilak, Lala Lajpat Rai and V.D. Savarkar who had come up with the Hindu-nation theory.

The belief that Hindus and Muslims should each have their separate nations found widespread support among middle-class Muslims across the subcontinent. After that no one, not Gandhiji, nor Nehru, Sardar Patel or Jinnah, could stop the process of religious cleansing of Hindus and Sikhs from Muslim-dominated areas. It may be recalled that as early as March 1947, Hindus and Sikhs were being driven out of towns and villages in north-west Punjab. There were communal riots in many cities in Punjab, including Lahore.

By 15 August 1947, the migration of Hindus

and Sikhs from Pakistan had become a bloody exodus. Sikhs and Hindus of east Punjab made sure that this was not going to be a one-way traffic: they drove out Muslims from east Punjab with double the violence. It was the most catastrophic exchange of populations in the history of mankind, leaving a million dead and tens of millions homeless. The aftermath was more barbaric than anything beasts could have done to each other.

I don't think either Pandit Nehru or Jinnah had imagined this level of violence. In any case both of them seemed to live in a dream world of their own—Jinnah had even hoped that he would go back to Bombay and live in his house there. The only person who did seem to comprehend the seriousness of Partition and all that followed was Mahatma Gandhi. He did not take part in any of the Independence celebrations in 1947. He remained quiet. When anti-Pakistan feelings were at fever pitch and the Indian government refused to honour its pledge to pay Pakistan Rs 55 crore, he went on a fast, forcing Patel and Nehru to keep their word.

Pointing accusing fingers at Nehru or Patel or Jinnah serves no purpose. They were helpless against the tidal waves of hatred generated by history, which were the real cause of the wars we have fought against Pakistan and the continuing conflict over the future of Kashmir.

The English-Language Paradox

I have often felt that language purists are the worst enemies of their mother tongue. The truth is that the more a language takes from others, the more it enriches itself. English is the richest language in the world because it has taken words from all languages with which it has come in contact. There is no dearth of examples. India has over two dozen languages. English has taken words from each one of them. Hindi, which is our national language, has not. Consequently, Hindi, which should have become our link language, has failed to do so, and the language that links all parts of the country remains English.

There seem to be two reasons for the failure of our intellectuals to change society. One is that all of them write in English, a language that barely 10 per cent of educated Indians can read and comprehend. The masses never get to know about them and what they are saying. The second and the more important factor was, and is, the fact that the vast majority of our countrymen look up to their gurus or godmen for guidance because they speak their language. And the mode of communication of these gurus and godmen is oral and not written.

Gurus have massive following, but their learning is limited to churning out accepted religious concepts unaffected by occidental learning. Most of their *pravachans* (lectures) are accompanied by hymn singing and, at times, dancing in ecstasy. Their congregations return to their homes content and at peace with themselves because they do not have to wrestle with new ideas. That is why caste distinctions persist, foeticide is widely practised and we continue to breed at a suicidal rate. Our gurus never deal with these serious problems that pose such a threat to our society.

To Prohibit Is to Promote

One way to ensure higher sales of something is to ban it. The case of prohibition of alcoholic drinks is as old as history; the ban on smoking is recent. Both have proved to be flops wherever they have been tried.

America went through many years of prohibition before it discovered it did not work. India tried it in fits and starts in different states and gave up after realizing that however stringent the laws, people addicted to drinking managed to get their hands on alcohol—if not legally, then through some spurious substitute which took their lives. Gujarat is the one state that has refused to learn lessons. It is not surprising then that people in Gujarat die regularly after drinking poisonous brew.

Drinking is not a vice, drunkenness is. All over the world, adults are allowed to drink when and what they like. It is only when they get drunk and misbehave that they are arrested. Drink like a gentleman or a lady; it is a civilized thing to do. It breaks the ice and encourages bonding. If England had no pubs, life in that country would become drab. All over Europe, the making of wine is a fine art. People have wine cellars in their homes and have their favourite wine with both meals. No one is any the worse for doing so.

Indians have been drinking since pre-Vedic times. The alcohol was mostly homemade stuff, and later, local brews like *arrack*, *mahua*, *tharra* and *feni* became a cottage industry. With the advent of the Europeans, the liquor industry developed, and we began to brew our own beers, distil whisky, gin and rum. In recent years, we have also started making wines. Vineyards have come up in Maharashtra and Karnataka. So we have our own red, white and rose wines as well as champagne. Many of them are as good as any imported wine, and are good enough to earn us foreign exchange.

Our aim should be to produce good-quality beverages with low alcohol content like lager, cider and wines—rather than spirits like whisky, gin, rum or *feni*—at low prices, which the poor can afford to buy. But will our stupid politicians ever listen?

Greed: The Deadliest Sin of All

Our ancestors made a list of five deadly sins: *kaam* (lust), *krodh* (anger), *lobh* (greed), *moh* (attachment) and *ahankaar* (pride). Of these, four take a deadly toll on the one who indulges in them, and marginally on their family and friends as well. However, greed (*lobh*) is the deadliest of the five sins. It not only diminishes the greedy in the eyes of his fellow beings but also deprives thousands of others of their hard-earned living. Very often it is greed that takes people down evil paths as they try to attain what they want.

What makes a person who has over hundreds of crores worth of assets—who eats the tastiest of food, drinks the headiest of wines, lives in a large mansion with a retinue of servants, has a fleet of limousines and gets everything he wants—want more? More real estate and more money in different banks? He should know he can't take it with him when he dies. Perhaps he wants to provide for his sons and daughters, grandchildren and descendants down many generations. He should know inherited wealth is unearned wealth and is soon frittered away in contentious litigation. He would die a happier man if he spent what he cannot use in building schools, colleges or hospitals for the poor.

If we give ourselves some time to think about the things we have done because of greed rather than need, we might realize where we have gone wrong. Our minds would be cleansed. This would help us to be better citizens, and better human beings.

When It Comes to Sex

Indians have it on their brains more than they have it in the right place but, as it happens, when you age, it automatically shifts from the groin to the head and you are obsessed with it. Sex is so integral and important to one's life that you cannot avoid thinking about it. It is something which is elemental, vital and far more important than other emotions like love or anger. And it expresses itself in weird ways. You cannot suppress it, that's why things like celibacy don't work. The desire to have multiple relationships is also human. I have written about the so-called happily married couple many times. Whether they do it or not, adultery is always at the back of the mind of both partners.

Human relationships are basically dictated by the desire for sex. Sex is at the root of so much of what people do to each other— whether it's what one hears from friends about their problems, or crimes of passion, or legal cases. I have realized that the relationships between man and woman can be so multiple and varied and take such weird forms sometimes. Some of them are quite unmentionable. But I feel one is being dishonest if one ignores sex, if one doesn't talk about it or write about it.

I have always believed that sex is more important than romance. Romance is a waste of energy—it takes up time and loses its lustre very soon. The same person becomes boring after a while and you lose interest in a person once bedded. Desire and its intensity, on the other hand, make a difference. If there's attraction on both sides, if the feelings are reciprocated and there's no holding back, then the encounter can lead to a very fulfilling affair.

There's too much sexual frustration in our country. This probably explains the rise in molestations and rapes. It's linked to sexual repression and hypocrisy—we Indians are very interested in sex, have the curiosity and the appetite but pretend to be very prudish and conservative. It's time we stopped withholding our urges and expressed ourselves. Or else it's bound to come out in some other form that might not be pleasant or desirable.

The Qualities of a President

I recently came across a delightful job description for the President of India on the front cover of *Thuglak* magazine, edited by the satirist Cho Ramaswamy. Translated, it read as follows:

* Excellent job opportunity for the old and infirm
* Nature of job: President of India
* Age: 35 and above. Preference will be given to candidates over 80
* Job content:

  i) Console people on Republic Day after the flag hoisting
  ii) Keep perusing mercy petitions from murderers without taking any decision
  iii) Travel abroad with family

* Salary: Rs 1,50,000 per month
* Perks: Space here not sufficient. Booklet with full list will be sent on payment of Rs 10 by crossed postal order

Most of our Presidents are forgotten soon after their term is over. A.P.J. Abdul Kalam is an exception. I've not the slightest doubt that he is the best President we have ever had. The reasons are simple: most of our Presidents were politicians who ended their careers in Rashtrapati Bhavan, and Indians do not have much respect for politicians.

Two of our Presidents, Radhakrishnan and Zakir Hussain, were academics. While Radhakrishnan was a scholar of Hinduism and a great orator, he did not practise what he preached. He indulged in cronyism and patronized people who did not deserve the honours he bestowed on them. Zakir Hussain was also a widely respected scholar. But he did very little besides discharging the routine duties expected of a President.

We also had our first woman President. But she too had a political background. What riled me most about her was that she subscribed to astrology.

What are the qualities one looks for in a President?

He or she should be financially clean and above nepotism.

The person must be principled and have a modern outlook.

He must not be a bigot.

He should be a brave man.

I believe Abdul Kalam, a scientist, had all these qualities. I hold him in high regard and have great respect for someone who believes in the following:

> A borderless society with no divisions of caste and community can only arise from borderless minds. It has taken centuries for our society to evolve into the present structure of caste and community. Love, patience, good laws and fair justice are the best instruments for our society to transform itself into a borderless community where hands that serve are better than lips that pray.
>
> —A.P.J. Abdul Kalam

The Highest Award

The Bharat Ratna, most recently awarded to Pandit Bhimsen Joshi, is the country's highest civilian award. I think this highest honour should be restricted to social workers and creative people like scientists, musicians and artists, and should never be given to retired or deceased politicians or civil servants.

WATCHING NATURE

Watching nature and observing the change of seasons has always been an important part of my daily routine. For many years I maintained a record of the natural phenomena I encountered every day. My nature-watching has been mostly restricted to the back garden of my house in Sujan Singh Park, but how much that little garden has taught me!

The garden is a rectangular plot of green enclosed on two adjacent sides by a barbed-wire fence covered by bougainvillaea of different colours. The other two sides are formed by my neighbour's apartment and mine; my neighbour has fenced himself off with a wall of hibiscus.

I have four old avocado trees that used to give me dozens of avocados every monsoon, and a tall eucalyptus smothered by purple bougainvillaea. My wife had a very utilitarian approach to gardening so we had a small patch of grass with some limes, oranges, grapefruit and pomegranate. She also had a section reserved for vegetables. I don't grow many flowers—a bush of gardenia, a few jasmines and a spray of raat ki rani. At one end of the garden is a birdbath that used to be shared by sparrows, crows, mynahs, kites, pigeons, babblers and a dozen stray cats.

Facing my apartment in front is a square lawn shared by all the residents of Sujan Singh Park. It has several trees of the ficus family, a chorisia (Mexican silk cotton tree) which bears large pink flowers in late autumn, and an old mulberry. I have a permanent view of this lawn from my sitting room window that's framed by a madhumalati creeper.

What perhaps accounts for the profusion of bird life in our locality are the numerous nurseries in the vicinity and the foliage of many old papdi trees. There are also lots of butterflies, beetles and bugs of different kinds. But over the years I have observed some changes. One, the disappearance of vultures, sparrows, frogs, fireflies and moths during the rainy season. There are no vultures or sparrows that come to my birdbath or garden any more.

There was a time when I spent Sunday mornings in winter in the outskirts of Delhi, armed with a pair of binoculars and Salim Ali's or Whistler's books on birds. My favourite haunts were the banks of the Yamuna behind Tilpat village, Surajkund and the ruins of Tughlaqabad Fort. It has been many years since I've been able to do that.

Winter in Delhi has become more unbearable for me with each passing year and I find myself feeling miserable. It is not entirely due to the weather. I remember, during my school days, we lived in a house on Jantar Mantar Road (which today is Kerala House). It had a marble fountain in the front garden. On some days in December and January, it was so cold the water froze to ice. We had fogs and heavy mists. I quite enjoyed the winter months. I don't do so any more. It's probably because I'm in my late nineties and my blood is not as warm as it used to be. I keep cheering myself up, saying, "'If winter comes, spring cannot be far behind.'" By Republic Day, 26 January, signs of spring are visible: all kinds of flowers are in full bloom in our parks and roundabouts and we start putting away our winter garments till late autumn. Till then, I have hot-water bottles in my bed, heaters glowing round the clock, log fires every evening. And misery all the time.

One phenomenon that baffles me is why many cities in the plains like Delhi, Amritsar and Chandigarh are colder than Shimla which is 6000 feet above sea level. And why Bhatinda freezes to zero degrees.

There was a time when people in Delhi wore overcoats, and other winter garments such as cardigans and sweaters were a must. Today you see hardly anyone wearing an overcoat; and woollen cardigans and sweaters are fast disappearing. This is due to thermal wear made of lightweight synthetic material like 'fleece' which seems to have revolutionized winter fashion. You can wear jackets, shirts and leggings made of these materials and need nothing more to ward off the chill. 'No weather is bad when you are suitably clad,' said Arthur Gutterman. I am as suitably clad as I can be, but still feel the winter chill, and don't look forward to this season as I once used to do.

I remember a time I looked forward to celebrating New Years' Eve by drinking, dancing and flirting, ushering in the New Year singing Auld Lang Syne at midnight. I spent many First of Januarys nursing hangovers with cups of black coffee and aspirins. I have not done this for many years. On New year's Eve, I go to bed by 10 p.m., latest, and barely hear my neighbours bursting crackers at midnight.

All our calendars are man-made. The only one that is followed around the world is the Roman one. Every community has their own new year, but New Year's Eve and the first day of January are celebrated universally as a new beginning. Making New Year resolutions is also the monopoly of the Roman calendar.

There was a time when I used to make resolutions to better myself. Year after year, I swore I would not malign people I hated. The resolution barely lasted a month before I resumed saying or writing exactly what I felt.

It is too late for me to become a better human being.

POETRY IS PRICELESS

Poetry has kept me company throughout my life. Apart from solace, it has given me great joy. There was a time I could recite English poetry for hours, all by rote. Then, Urdu poetry took over and I memorized large chunks of Ghalib, Iqbal, Hafeez, Faiz and Ahmad Faraz, and the English poets faded from my memory. I would start with a few lines and not be able to recall those that followed. I felt guilty, which is why I now keep my favourite anthologies of English poetry—and I have many of them—close at hand. I also have the King James Bible by my bedside, the Granth Sahib and various translations, including my own, of Urdu poetry. I like to dip into these every now and then. There is great wisdom in the poetry I love and read. I recite my favourite lines whenever I get a chance. I have always loved the music and rhythm that

poetry offers. There are poems for every mood
and emotion. Here are some of my favourite
lines of verse, starting with the Urdu poets:

Mirza Ghalib
(1796–1869)

I.

Naqsh fariyadee hai kis kee shoukhee-e-
        tehreer ka
Kaaghazee hai pairahan har paikar-e-
        tasveer ka

A picture speaks for itself, what learned
    exposition does it need?
The paper on which it is painted is only its
    outer garment: it tells its own tale
    indeed.

II.

Go haath ko jumbish naheen aankhon mein to
        dam hai
Rehney do abhee saaghar-o-meena merey aagey

Though I can no longer stretch my hands
    I still have life's sparkle in my eyes.
Let the jug of wine and cup remain before
    me where they lie.

III.

Ishq sey tabeeyat ney zeest ka mazaa paaya
Dard kee davaa payee dard-e-la-davaa paaya

Love gave me the lust for living—to ease
     my pain it gave me something for
     sure;
It gave me such pain that nothing can
     cure.

IV.

Mehrbaan hokey bulaalo mujhey chaaho jis
     vaqt
Main gayaa vaqt naheen hoon ki phir aa
     bhee na sakoon

Have mercy and send for me any time
     you so desire;
Time gone is forever gone it's true—I
     am not time, I can always return
     to you.

Faiz Ahmad Faiz
(1911–1984)

I.

Raat yoon dil mein teree khoyee hue yaad aaee
Jaisey veeraney mein chupkey sey bahaar aa
    jaaye
Jaisey sahraaon mein hauley sey chaley baad-e-
    naseem
Jaisey beemaar ko bevajah qaraar aa jaaye

Last night the lost memory of you stole
    into my mind
Stealthily as spring steals into a wilderness
As on desert wastes a gentle breeze begins
    to blow
As in one sick beyond hope, hope begins
    to grow.

II.

Mujh sey pehlee see mohabbat meree mehboob
    na maang
Main ney samjha thha ki too hai to
    darakhshaan hai hayaat
Tera gham hai to gham-e-dehr ka jhagra kya
    hai

*Teree soorat sey hai aalam mei bahaaron ko
     sabaat*

Too jo mil jaaye to taqdeer nagoon ho jaaye

*Yoon na thha mainey faqat chaahaa thha
     yoon ho jaaye*

*Aur bhee dukh hain zamaaney mein muhabbat
     key siva*

*Raahatein aur bhee hain wasl kee raahat key
     sivaa*

*Anginat sadiyon key taareek baheemaanaa
     tilism*

Resham-o-atlas-o-kamkhwaab key bunvaaye huey

*Jaa-ba-jaa biktey huey koocha-o-baazaar mein
     jism*

Beloved, do not ask me for the love I had
     before

Then I had thought life was worth living
     because of you

If I was in pain, I did not care what others
     went through

Your face gave the world assurance of
     springs to come.

Besides your eyes, to me the world meant
     nothing

And I would triumph over everyone if I
     won you.

It was not meant to be, I only wished it so
There are sorrows other than love's sorrow
There are joys other than the joy of union
　　with the beloved.
Countless centuries have witnessed
　　tragedies
Interwoven in fabrics of silk in bazaars and
　　in the market place
Smothered in dust and soaked in blood
　　and gore.

Apart from Urdu poetry, here are some more
favourites that I turn to often, from a variety of
sources—English poems, verses from the Sikh
scriptures, and from the Old Testament's Book
of Job and Psalms of David:

'The Revelation', Coventry Patmore

An idle poet, here and there,
Looks round him; but, for all the rest,
The world, unfathomably fair,
Is duller than a witling's jest.

Love wakes men, once a lifetime each;
They lift their heavy lids, and look;
And, lo, what one sweet page can teach,
They read with joy, then shut the book.
And give some thanks, and some
          blaspheme,
And most forget; but, either way,
That and the child's unheeded dream
Is all the light of all their day.

From 'Desiderata', Max Ehrmann

You are a child of the universe,
no less than the trees and the stars;
you have a right to be here.
And whether or not it is clear to you,
no doubt the universe is unfolding as it
          should.

From the 'Japji' (The Morning Prayer),
Adi Granth, Nanak

There is one God.
He is the supreme truth.

He, the creator,
Is without fear and without hate.
He, the omnipresent,
Pervades the universe.
He is not born,
Nor does He die to be born again.

From 'Vaisakh', Bara Maha, Nanak

Nanak says: 'Where seek you the Lord?
Whom do you await?
You have not far to go to find Him.
He is within you, you are His mansion.
If your body and soul yearn for the Lord,
The Lord shall love you and Vaisakh shall
      be beautiful.'

From the Adi Granth, Nanak

There are five prayers
Each with a time and a name of its own.
First, truthfulness.
Second, to take only what is your due.
Third, goodwill towards all.
Fourth, pure intentions;
And praise of God, the fifth.

Let good acts be your creed: persevere
    with them;
Then proclaim you are a Muslim.
O Nanak, the more false the man
The more evil his power.

Job, 1:21

Naked came I from my mother's womb,
    and naked shall I return tither;
The Lord gave, and the Lord hath taken
    away;
Blessed be the name of the Lord.

Psalms, 23 (A Psalm of David)

The Lord is my shepherd; I shall not want.
He maketh me to lie down in green
    pastures: he leadeth me beside the
    still waters.
He restoreth my soul: he leadeth me in
    the paths of righteousness for his
    name's sake.

Yea, though I walk through the valley
of the shadow of death, I will fear
no evil: for thou art with me; thy
rod and thy staff, they comfort me.
Thou preparest a table before me in the
presence of mine enemies; thou
anointest my head with oil; my cup
runneth over.
Surely goodness and mercy shall follow me
all the days of my life; and I will dwell
in the house of the Lord forever.

From 'Ode to a Nightingale', John Keats

Darkling I listen; and, for many a time
I have been half in love with easeful Death,
Call'd him soft names in many a mused
rhyme,
To take into the air my quiet breath;
Now more than ever seems it rich to die,
To cease upon the midnight with no pain,
While thou art pouring forth thy soul
abroad

In such an ecstasy!
Still wouldst thou sing, and I have ears
    in vain—
To thy high requiem become a sod.

From 'The World Is Too Much With Us',
William Wordsworth

The world is too much with us; late and
    soon,
Getting and spending, we lay waste our
    powers;
Little we see in Nature that is ours;
We have given our hearts away, a sordid
    boon!

From 'Oft in the Stilly Night', Thomas Moore

Oft, in the stilly night,
Ere Slumber's chain has bound me,
Fond Memory brings the light

Of other days around me;
The smiles, the tears
Of boyhood's years,
The words of love then spoken;
The eyes that shone,
Now dimm'd and gone,
The cheerful hearts now broken!

DEALING WITH DEATH

There is a passage in the Mahabharat which says that the greatest miracle of life is that while we know that death is inevitable, no one really believes that he too will die one day. We humans have always been obsessed with death and dying. I tried to come to terms with it early on but found myself, as the Dhammapada says, like a fish thrown on dry land, thrashing about trying to free itself from the power of death.

I once asked the Dalai Lama how one should face death and he advised meditation. The one time I met Acharya Rajneesh in Bombay, I spoke to him about my fears and asked him how best to cope with them. He told me the only way to overcome the fear of death was to expose myself to the dying and the dead. I had been doing this on my own for many years. I rarely attended weddings but made it a point to go to funerals. I would sit by dead relatives and often went to the cremation ground at Nigambodh Ghat to watch pyres being lit and corpses go up in flames. It acted as a catharsis: it cleansed me of pettiness and vanity, and helped me take life's setbacks in my stride. I would take stock of my life, be thankful for what I had. I would return home at peace with myself. However, it did not help me overcome the fear of death. On the contrary, I often had trouble sleeping, and had nightmares set off by what I had seen.

I think the reason I used to dread death and fear it so much was because I had no idea where I'd be afterwards. My inability to accept the existence of God negates the possibility of a life after death and the concept of rebirth. The Bhagavad Gita assures us: 'For certain is death for the born, and certain is birth for the dead; therefore, over the inevitable thou shouldst not grieve.' I accept the first part, for I know it to be true; I have no evidence of the second part. There is no proof of an afterlife. So it's the dissolving into nothingness that I feared. Tom Stoppard summed up what I felt when he wrote: '[Death] is the absence of presence, nothing more . . . the endless time of never coming back . . . a gap you can't see, and when the wind blows through it, it makes not sound.' And Paul Valery, when he said: 'Death speaks to us with a deep voice but has nothing to say.' I took comfort in these lines by Tennyson:

> Sunset and evening star,
> And one clear call for me!
> And may there be no moaning of the bar,
> When I put out to sea . . .
> Twilight and evening bell,
> And after that the dark!
> And may there be no sadness or farewell,
> When I embark . . .

As far as I'm concerned, death is the final full stop. Beyond it there is nothing. It's a void that no one has been able to penetrate. It has no tomorrows. 'What is the world to a man when his wife is a widow?' goes an Irish saying.

The process of dying begins the moment we are born. Death is the only thing in life we can be certain of. It is inevitable. Why, then, are we so scared of it? Would it help if we knew when we are going to die? I don't think so. I don't think we'd be able to handle it. It would make us even more depressed. We'd waste the little time we have worrying about the end.

I realized early on that I have only one life to live and, not knowing when it will come to an end, decided to get as much out of it as I could. I have lived life to the full. I have travelled the world, indulged my senses, basked in the beauty of nature and enjoyed all it has had to offer. I have sampled the best food and drink, listened to good music and made love to beautiful women. I have always made the most of the time that I have been given.

These days, I think of death more than ever before but I have stopped worrying or brooding about it. I think of those I have lost; past sweethearts whose memories steal back into my mind; loved ones I shall see no more. I wonder where they are. Will I see them again? What next? I don't have the answers. To quote Omar Khayyam:

> Into this Universe, and Why not knowing
> Nor Whence, like Water willy-nilly
> flowing . . .

and

> There was a Door to which I found no
> Key:
> There was a Veil through which I could
> not see:
> Some little Talk awhile of Me and Thee
> There seemed—and then no more of
> Thee and Me.

All my contemporaries—whether here, in England or in Pakistan—they're all gone. I don't know when my time will come but I don't fear death anymore. What I dread is the day I go blind or am incapacitated because of old age—that's what I fear. I'd rather die than live like that. I'm a burden enough on my daughter Mala and don't want to be more of a burden on her.

All that I hope for is that when death comes to me it comes quickly, without much pain, like slipping away in sound sleep. Till then I'll keep working and living each day as it comes. I'm still writing and am able to keep up with my reading. The problem is I can't keep still. I have to keep busy. These lines of Iqbal come to mind:

> *Baagh-e-bahisht sey mujhey hukm-e safar diya*
> *thha kyon?*
> *Kaar-e-Jahaan daraaz hai, ab mera intezaar*
> *kar*

> (Why did you order me out of the garden
> of paradise?
> I have a lot left to do; now you wait for me.)

So I often tell Bade Mian, as I refer to him, that he's got to wait for me as I still have work to finish.

I actually believe in the Jain philosophy that death ought to be celebrated. I had even written my own obituary in 1943 when I was in my twenties. It later appeared in a collection of short stories, titled *Posthumous*. In the piece I imagined the *Tribune* announcing news of my death on its front page with a small photograph. The headline would read: 'Sardar Khushwant Singh Dead'. And then in somewhat smaller print: 'We regret to announce the sudden death of Sardar Khushwant Singh at 6 p.m. last evening. He leaves behind a young widow, two infant children and a large number of friends and admirers ... Amongst those who called at the late sardar's residence were the PA to the chief justice, several ministers, and judges of the High Court.'

I had to cope with death when I lost my wife. Being an agnostic I could not find solace in religious rituals. Being a loner essentially, I discouraged friends and relatives from coming to condole with me. I spent the first night alone sitting in my chair in the dark. At times I broke down but soon recovered my composure. A couple of days later I resumed my usual routine, working from dawn to dusk. That took my mind off the stark reality of having to live alone in an empty home for the rest of my days. When friends persisted in calling and upset my equilibrium, I went off to Goa to be by myself.

I used to be keen on a burial because with a burial you give back to the earth what you have taken. Now I would like it to be the electric crematorium. I had asked the management of the Bahai faith if I could be buried in their enclosure. Initially they agreed but then they came up with all kinds of conditions and rules. I had wanted to be buried in one corner with a peepal tree next to my grave. After agreeing to this, the management later said that that wouldn't be possible—that that my grave would be in the middle of a row and not in a corner. I wasn't okay with that—even though I know that once you are dead it makes no difference. But I was keen to be buried in a corner. They also told me that they would chant some prayers, which again I couldn't agree with because I don't believe in religion or in religious rituals of any kind.

And since I have no faith in God, or in the Day of Judgement, or in the theory of reincarnation, I have to come to terms with the complete full stop. I have been criticized for not sparing even the dead, for being critical of people who have died, but then death does not sanctify a person, and if I find the person had been corrupt, I write about it and talk about it even after he's gone.

When my time comes, I don't want to make an ass of myself. I don't want to be a burden to anyone. I don't want to cry for help or ask

God to forgive me for my sins. I'd like to go like my father did. He died a few minutes after he'd had his evening Scotch. I'd like to have one last drink before heading out.

Above all, I want to go like a man without any regrets or grievances against anyone. Allama Iqbal expressed it so beautifully in a couplet:

Nishaan-e-mard-e Momin ba too goyam?
Choon marg aayad, tabassum bar lab-e-ost

(You ask me for the signs of a man of
    faith?
When death comes to him, he has a smile
    on his lips.)

TWELVE TIPS TO LIVE LONG AND BE HAPPY

I believe genes play a very important role in determining one's lifespan. Children of long-living parents are likely to have long lives. However, there are ways in which one can live life to the full, and spend the time that we have been given in a healthy and fruitful manner.

1. Try and play a game—whether it's tennis or squash, badminton or golf, a round is good for you. Or exercise regularly: an hour of brisk walking, swimming or running is as good.

2. If you cannot do any of these, get yourself a vigorous massage at least once a day. Powerful hands moving over your body from skull to toes improves blood circulation.

3. Cut down on your intake of food and drink. Maintain a strict routine for meals.

I have breakfast at 6.30 a.m., lunch at noon, a drink at 7 p.m. and supper at 8 p.m. Start your day with a glass of fruit juice. (Guava juice is better than any other.)

4. A single peg of single malt whiskey in the evening is good for your appetite.

5. Before you eat dinner say to yourself: 'Don't eat much.' Try and eat alone and in silence.

6. Stick to one kind of vegetable or meat followed by a pinch of chooran. (Idli-dosa is a healthier option as it is easier to digest.)

7. Never allow yourself to be constipated. Keep your bowels clean by whatever means you can: laxatives, enemas, glycerine suppositories.

8. Keep a healthy bank balance for peace of mind. It does not have to be in crores but enough for your future needs and the possibility of illness or failing health.

9. Don't lose your temper, and do laugh often.

10. Don't tell a lie.

11. Give generously. It will cleanse your soul. Remember, you cannot take what you have with you.

12. Instead of whiling away your time praying, take up a hobby: gardening, music, helping children or those who are in need. Remember: always keep busy. Keep both your mind and hands working.

HUMOUR IS A LETHAL WEAPON

We Indians take life far too seriously and consider far too many things sacred. Worst of all, we don't have the ability to laugh at ourselves. And people who can't do that can never cultivate a genuine sense of humour. It doesn't take much wit to be regarded as a humorist in a nation as humourless as ours. It is no surprise then that my joke books have sold more than any other of my writings and that the first item most readers of my column look at is the last one that I usually reserve for a joke or humorous anecdote. I find it funny that joke books are bestsellers in a country without a sense of humour.

However, we are not entirely without humour. While we can't laugh at ourselves, we are quick to laugh at other people. India has a long tradition of making fun of its kings and queens, ministers and generals and other people in power. Court jesters and clowns were allowed to mock them and speak their mind. They were tolerated because this was the only way the rulers got the real picture: what was really going on in the country and what was being said about them behind their backs. And the more tyrannical the rule, the more underground humour it generated.

While the legacies of Birbal, Tenali Raman and Gopal Bhar have not been lost, the largest number of jokes in our country centre on ethnic stereotypes and communities. Interestingly, most of these are made up by the communities themselves. And while it's funny if they narrate them, they are very touchy and sensitive if the jokes are narrated by others. The best of our jokes remain a part of an oral tradition and are rarely seen in print. We are also a cowardly nation and are very scared of lawsuits.

I've never taken anything very seriously, least of all myself. I wish more journalists and writers would use humour. It is the most lethal weapon. Unfortunately they tend to use anger instead.

Humour—and laughter—is a leveller. It is also good for the soul. It keeps you healthy and is one of the keys to a longer life.

Once on a visit to Sweden, I was introduced to a Professor Lund who was due to go on a lecture tour of India. Lund is a common name in Scandinavia. After a few drinks I confided in him that when being introduced to Indian audiences he should be prepared for a few sniggers. He took it very calmly and replied: 'That is very interesting. I was in a similar predicament when a lady professor from your country came here to deliver some lectures and I had to introduce her. Her name was Miss Das. In Swedish, the word "doss" means shit.'

Two friends, Santa Singh and Banta Singh, were always boasting about their parents' achievements.

Santa Singh: Have you heard of the Suez Canal?

Banta Singh: Yes, I have.

Santa Singh: Well, my father dug it.

Banta Singh: That's nothing. Have you heard of the Dead Sea?

Santa Singh: Yes.

Banta Singh: Well, my father killed it.

After the stock scam and the subsequent collapse of the stock market, a businessman was asked by his friend if he too had done any trading.

'Of course I did,' the businessman said.

'What were you? A bull or a bear?'

'An ass.'

I have been the recipient of honours like the Padma Bhushan and Padma Vibhushan, but it will be my lasting regret that I never achieved the eminence of a George Bush, P. Chidambaram or L.K. Advani to have had the honour of having a shoe flung at me.

When Bhindranwale was on a rampage in Punjab, I wrote articles criticizing him and warning Sikhs against the spurious demand for Khalistan. He put me on his hit list but his *sopariwala* failed to get me. But I received a lot of hate mail. One letter from Canada became a memento. It had the foulest Punjabi abuse, accusing me of all manner of incestuous relationships. It was written in Gurmukhi. Only the address was in English: 'Bastard Khushwant Singh, India'. I was most impressed by the efficiency of the Indian postal service in locating the address of the one and only bastard in the country. I went around showing it to all my friends with great glee until my wife tore it up in utter disgust. What a loss!

But the Oscar of all the hate mail I have received goes to Uma Bharati. She was very *gussa* with me. She has a volatile temper and

this time I was at the receiving end. I had
ascribed the venomous utterances of four ladies
(including her) against Muslims, to sexual
frustration. In a letter written in florid Hindi
she accused me of misogyny. I wish that was
true because it is my liking for women which
has made me notorious. I have little doubt that
if I had been anywhere near her, she would
have given me a resounding slap on the face, as
she once did to one of her supporters in a fit
of uncontrolled rage—and would not have
bothered to make amends by kissing me as she
did her supporter. Instead, with the letter she
sent a vial of *gaumutra* (cow's urine) to drink. I
don't subscribe to urine therapy. The very thought
of taking urine, be it Morarji Desai's, hers, my
own or that of the sacred cow, brings vomit to
my throat. I flushed it down the toilet.

When Babu Jagjivan Ram was the minister for
railways, he once piloted a bill suggesting free

rail travel for MPs' spouses. Atal Bihari Vajpayee, the bachelor MP, asked the minister if a bachelor was allowed to take a companion with him for free. Jagjivan Ram's reply: 'The Honourable Member forgets that the legislation is for spouse, not spice!'

A man goes to the doctor complaining of loss of hearing. The doctor examines him and says he wants to fix the fellow with a new hearing aid.

'This is the finest hearing aid now being manufactured. I wear one myself,' the doctor said.

'What kind is it? the man asked.

'Half past four.'

She: Here's your ring. I can't marry you because I love someone else.

He: Who is he?

She (*nervously*): You're not going to try and kill him?

He: No, but I'll try to sell him the ring.

President Zail Singh was operated on in the same Texan hospital as his predecessor, Sanjiva Reddy. When taken to the operating theatre, the chief surgeon asked the President: 'Are you ready?'

'No, I am not,' he replied. 'I am Zail Singh.'

A couple was celebrating the birth of their first child, a son. After the party was over, the husband turned to the wife: 'My dear, I think one son is enough for us. So if you don't mind I'd like to have a vasectomy. What do you think?'

'Do as you wish,' the wife replied. 'You have

your vasectomy now. I'll have my tubes tied
after I have my third child.'

The late Pakistani President General Zia, while
driving around Islamabad, came across long
queues of Pakistanis outside several embassies,
waiting for entry permits and visas to go abroad.
He got out of the car and joined one of the
queues to find out why so many people were
wanting to leave the country. No sooner did
they see their President with them than they
left the queue and returned to their homes.
President Zia asked them why they were leaving.
They said: 'If you are leaving Pakistan, there's
no need for us to go.'

'I am the most unfortunate man in the world!
My kismet is ruined!' cried Lala Dhani Ram,
slapping his forehead.

'Why, Lalaji? What's the matter?'

'My daughter's gone and married that good-for-nothing fellow who doesn't know how to drink or gamble.'

'You call that bad kismet? You should consider yourself lucky to have a son-in-law who doesn't drink or gamble!'

'Who said he doesn't drink or gamble? He does both. He just does not know how to do them.'

A couple hired a new chauffeur. The woman asked him to take her out shopping and she was very shaken by the experience. When she returned home she pleaded with her husband, 'Please, dear, you must sack him at once. He is so rash, he nearly killed me three times this morning!'

'Darling, let's not be so hasty,' the husband replied. 'We should give him another chance.'

It all started during my recent summer vacation in Kasauli. I woke up one night with a queasy feeling in my stomach. Half asleep, I tottered to the loo to rid myself of my sleep-breaker. When I got up from the lavatory seat to flush out the contents, I was shocked to see I had passed a lot of blood with my stool. 'Shit!' I said to myself, suddenly wide awake. The rest of the night was wasted in contemplation of the end. I had had a reasonable innings, close to scoring a century, so no regrets on that score. Was I creating a self-image of heroism in the face of death? That vanished on the following day as more blood flowed out of my belly.

I asked my friend Dr Santosh Kutty of the Central Research Institute (CRI) to drop in for a drink in the evening. Over a glass of Scotch, he heard me out. When I finished, he asked me: 'Have you been eating *chukandar*?' I admitted I'd had beetroot salad the day before.

'It could be that,' he suggested. 'It is the same colour as human blood. Or it could be

nature's way of reducing high blood pressure—
bleeding through the nose or arse. Or it could
be a polyp, or piles, or . . .' He did not use the
word but I understood he meant cancer. 'Let
me examine your rectum.'

'You'll do no such thing,' I rasped. 'I'd
rather die than show my rectum to anyone.'
He paused and continued, 'It would be wise to
have an endoscopy. It will clear all doubts. We
don't have the facility in Kasauli. You can have
it done at PGI in Chandigarh or in Delhi. The
sooner the better.'

I opted for Delhi, to be with my family. And
rang up my friend Nanak Kohli to send up his
Mercedes Benz to take me down. I looked up
my dictionary to find out exactly what
polyp and endoscopy meant. One is a kind of
sea urchin-like growth in the lower part of the
intestine, the other an instrumental
examination of one's innards. I spent the rest
of the day drafting in my mind farewell letters
to my near and dear ones. Nothing mawkish
or sentimental, but in the tone of one who

couldn't care less about his fate, something they could quote in my obituaries: he went like a man, with a smile on his face, etc.

The next morning, my son Rahul and I drove back to Delhi. The first thing I did was to ask Dr I.P.S. Kalra, who lives in the neighbouring block, to come over. Dr Kalra is a devout believer of miracles performed by Waheguru. He has been our doctor for over half a century and has treated several members of my extended family in their last days on earth, until their journey to the electric crematorium. Since I am a lot older than him, he addresses me as Veerji (elder brother). He took my blood pressure; it was higher than normal. He heard my bloody tale and straightaway fixed an appointment with Dr S.K. Jain, Delhi's leading endoscopist.

The next evening, accompanied by Kalra, Rahul and my daughter Mala, I presented myself at Dr Jain's swanky clinic in Hauz Khas Enclave. All white marble, spotlessly clean, and with the obligatory statuette of Lord Ganapati with a garland of fresh marigold flowers around his neck sitting above the receptionist's desk. Since I was the first patient of the many he had to examine that evening, I was conducted immediately to his operating room.

I can tell you that endoscopy strips your self-esteem and any dignity you may have. I was ordered to take off my salwar-kameez, given an overall to wear, and ordered to lie down. Dr Jain took my BP and proceeded to insert an endoscope up my rectum. At times the pain was excruciating. It went on for an hour. When it was over, Dr Kalra ordered me: 'Veerji, *pudd maro*—kill a fart, you'll feel easier.' I refused to oblige and instead went to the lavatory to get rid of the wind the nervous tension had created inside me.

Dr Jain pronounced the verdict: 'No polyp, no cancer, only internal piles which bleed because of high BP. It is nature's way of bringing it down.' As a parting gift, he gave Mala a filmed version of all that had transpired—from my bottom being bared to the muck inside my belly. As if that was not enough, when asked about his father's health, Rahul told everyone, 'Pop has piles.' There is something romantic about cancer; polyp is like a plop sound produced by a frog leaping into a stagnant pool; but haemorrhoids have no romance attached to them; they are simply a miserable man's piles. Many well-wishers called to enquire how my endoscopy had gone and how I felt about the whole exercise. My reply was standard: 'I feel buggered.'

EPITAPH

On Independence Day 2012 I turned ninety-eight. Being aware of my state of health, I know that I will not write another book. Even the chances of my continuing with my biweekly columns, which I have been doing without a break for almost fifty years, appear bleak. The truth is that I want to die. I have lived long enough. Whatever I wanted to do in life, I have done. So what is the point of hanging on to life with nothing whatsoever left to do?

How would I like to be remembered when I am gone? I would like to be remembered as someone who made people smile. A few years ago, I wrote my own epitaph:

> Here lies one who spared neither man
>   nor God
> Waste not your tears on him, he was a sod

Writing nasty things he regarded as great
  fun
Thank the Lord he is dead, this son of a
  gun.

—Khushwant Singh

Also by Khushwant Singh

THE SUNSET CLUB

The Sunset Club **is Khushwant Singh at his best—as a
storyteller, a chronicler of our times, a nature lover and an
irreverent sage.**

Meet the members of the Sunset Club: Pandit Preetam Sharma,
Nawab Barkatullah Baig and Sardar Boota Singh. Friends for
over forty years, they are now in their eighties. Every evening, at
the sunset hour, they sit together on a bench in Lodhi Gardens
to exchange news and views on the events of the day, talking
about everything from love, lust, sex and scandal to religion
and politics. As he follows a year in the lives of the three men
Khushwant Singh brings his characters vibrantly to life, with his
piquant portrayals of their fantasies and foibles, his unerring ear
for dialogue and his genius for capturing the flavour and texture
of everyday life in their households.

Interwoven with this compelling human story is another
chronicle—of a year in the life of India, as the country goes
through the cycle of seasons, the tumult of general elections,
violence, natural disasters and corruption in high places. In turn
ribald and lyrical, poignant and profound, *The Sunset Club* is a
deeply moving exploration of friendship, sexuality, old age and
infirmity; a joyous celebration of nature; an insightful portrait of
India's paradoxes and complexities.

Fiction
Rs 250

ABSOLUTE KHUSHWANT: THE LOW-DOWN ON LIFE, DEATH AND MOST THINGS IN BETWEEN

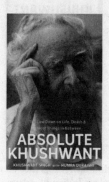

'I would like to be remembered as someone who made people smile.'

One of the great icons of our time, Khushwant Singh, 95, is a man of contradictions. An agnostic who's well-versed in the holy scriptures; a vocal champion of free speech who supported the Emergency; a 'dirty old man' who sees 'the world in a grain of sand and beauty in a wild flower'.

Born in 1915 in pre-Partition Punjab, Khushwant Singh has been witness to almost all the major events in modern Indian history and has known most of the figures who have shaped it. In a career spanning over six decades as writer, editor and journalist, his views have been provocative and controversial, but they have also been profound, deeply perceptive and always compelling. Khushwant Singh has never been less than honest.

In *Absolute Khushwant*, India's grand old man of letters tells us about his life, his loves and his work. He writes on happiness, faith and honesty. And, for the first time, about his successes and failures, his strengths and weaknesses, his highs and lows. He tells us what makes him tick and the secret of his longevity; he confesses his deepest fears and what he holds dear. He writes about sex, marriage, worship and death; the people he's admired and detested. With personal anecdotes and rare photographs, *Absolute Khushwant* is uncompromising, moving and straight from the heart.

Non-fiction
Rs 250

CLASSIC KHUSHWANT SINGH

**This omnibus edition brings together all of Singh's novels—
four classics of modern Indian literature:** *Train to Pakistan, I
Shall Not Hear the Nightingale, Delhi* **and** *Burial at Sea.*

First published in 1956, *Train to Pakistan* is a timeless
classic of modern Indian fiction.

~

I Shall Not Hear the Nightingale is widely acclaimed as
Khushwant Singh's finest novel.

~

Delhi is Khushwant Singh's bawdy, irreverent magnum
opus, about an ageing reprobate who travels through
time, space and history to 'discover' his beloved city.

~

Comic, tender and erotic by turns, *Burial at Sea* is
vintage Khushwant Singh.

Fiction Omnibus
Rs 499

THE PORTRAIT OF A LADY: COLLECTED STORIES

'A Khushwant Singh short story is not flamboyant but modest, restrained, well-crafted . . . perhaps his greatest gift as a writer is a wonderful particularity of description'—*London*

Khushwant Singh first established his reputation as a writer through the short story. His stories—wry, poignant, erotic and, above all, human—bear testimony to his remarkable range and his ability to create an unforgettable world.

Spanning over half a century, this volume contains all the short stories Khushwant Singh has ever written, including the delightfully tongue-in-cheek 'The Maharani of Chootiapuram', written in 2008.

> 'Khushwant's stories enthrall . . . [He has] an ability akin to that of Somerset Maugham . . . the ability to entertain intelligently'—*India Today*

> 'His stories are better than [those of] any Indian writing in English'—*Times of India*

> '*The Collected Short Stories* leaves the readers in a delightful, inebriated trance'—*Sunday Chronicle*

Anthology
Rs 350

TRUTH, LOVE AND A LITTLE MALICE

Born in 1915 in pre-Partition Punjab, Khushwant Singh, perhaps India's most widely read and controversial writer, has been witness to most of the major events in modern Indian history—from Independence and Partition to the Emergency and Operation Blue Star—and has known many of the figures who have shaped it. With clarity and candour, he writes of leaders like Jawaharlal Nehru and Indira Gandhi, the terrorist Jarnail Singh Bhindranwale, the talented and scandalous painter Amrita Sher-Gil, and everyday people who became butchers during Partition.

Writing of his own life, too, Khushwant Singh remains unflinchingly forthright. He records his professional triumphs and failures as a lawyer, journalist, writer and member of Parliament; the comforts and disappointments in his marriage of over sixty years; his first, awkward sexual encounter; his phobia of ghosts and his fascination with death; the friends who betrayed him, and also those whom he failed.

> 'Khushwant on Khushwant is . . . irresistible . . . such is his skill as a writer—simple, lucid, unpretentious—that oft-known episodes are given a new lease of life . . . this book has been well worth the wait'—*India Today*

> *Truth, Love & a Little Malice* [has] much that is new and exciting and memorable—written with frankness and honesty'—*Book Review*

> 'Singh's reminiscences about the famous men and women he has known makes for thrilling voyeuristic reading. He has a way of observing other people and telling a story that is almost unmatched'—*Times of India*

> 'A blunt and honest account . . . laced with a little peg of malice and single malt'—*Business India* user reviews

Autobiography
Rs 395